The Cancer Crusade's

Little Book
of
Hope & Humor

Nov. 19, 2008

To Julie with love & prayers
for a complete recovery.

Ted & Juanita

The Cancer Crusade's

Little Book
of
Hope & Humor

Roger & Kathy Cawthon

Ruby ❖ Press
Hampton, Virginia

**The Cancer Crusade's
Little Book of Hope & Humor**

Roger and Kathy Cawthon

Published by:
Ruby ❖ Press
Hampton, Virginia

Printed in the United States of America

Cover design and inside layout: www.TheBookProducer.com
Illustrations by JasonLove.com

ISBN 978-0-9770773-1-1

I don't feel no ways tired;
I've come too far from where I started from.
Nobody told me that the road would be easy;
I don't believe He brought me this far
   to leave me.

Reverend James Cleveland

I'm a little wounded, but I am not slain;
I will lay me down to bleed a while;
Then I'll rise and fight again.

John Dryden

Authors' Note

For the sake of clarity and for ease of reading, these affirmations are written in the first person from Kathy's viewpoint unless otherwise noted. All of the experiences and the telling of them, however, are shared by both authors.

Dedication

This book is dedicated with much peace and many healing prayers to everyone whose life has been touched by cancer. Remember that you are never alone. You are warriors in an army of millions. Fight on.

Contents

"I get up. I walk. I fall down.
Meanwhile, I keep dancing."
~Rabbi Hillel~

Introduction

At the relatively young age of 44, we were both – husband and wife – diagnosed with life-threatening cancers within six weeks of one another. There was no history of cancer of any kind in either of our families.

This occurrence was so unusual that one of our doctors said we had a better chance of winning the lottery. After we recovered from the initial shock of our diagnoses, we began to question why, if this was indeed such a rare thing, it had happened to us. If something so extraordinary had to happen to us, why couldn't it have been the lottery instead of cancer?

The answer began to reveal itself over the course of the next few years. During that time, we received excellent medical care from our surgeons, oncologists, treatment nurses and other medical professionals. We were cared for at an outstanding hospital and at a first-rate oncology clinic. Our treatment teams and facilities were the very best. We received cutting edge therapies for our diseases, and we began the long, slow process of recovery.

But there was something missing, something as vital to the healing of our spirits as surgery and drugs and radiation had been to the healing of our bodies. That something was the support and camaraderie of other survivors, other people who knew.

Don't misunderstand. We had lots of compassionate, loving support from our close-knit families and amazing friends. We had many welcome visitors and phone calls, and almost daily deliveries of cards and casseroles. But as much as our family members and friends loved us and wanted to take away our grief, anger and fear, they didn't know where to begin.

They could cry with us (and they did) and they could pray for us (and they did) and they could run errands and help with the housework and all of those practical things that needed doing (and they did all of these), but they couldn't know how it felt to sit down in a chair to receive an infusion of chemotherapy drugs or have a catheter inserted in their chests or lie partially naked on a cold, steel table, alone in a radiation therapy room except for huge machines making whirring noises and sudden, jerky movements. They couldn't know how it felt to have their hair fall out in fistfuls or laugh and cry and throw up all at the same time or wake in the middle of the night craving scrambled eggs. And they couldn't know how it felt to suddenly be acutely, painfully aware that they might not see another birthday or Christmas.

No one could know these things, we realized as our recoveries progressed, no one except others who had been where we were. Yes, there were a few so-called "support groups" in our community, but they were badly facilitated or not facilitated at all. Going to one of their meetings left us feeling even more hopeless and depressed than before.

And that's when the answer to the "Why us?" question began to reveal itself.

When this part of our journey was behind us, we could be there for others who were just beginning their own journeys, to help in whatever small way we could. Kathy could write about our experiences, and Roger could make jokes about them. After all, those were the things we loved to do, so couldn't we find a way to do something good with them?

The Cancer Crusade was born. We began sending out a free, monthly newsletter entitled "The Cancer Connection" via e-mail to an initial subscriber list of 42. The response was so great that the list quickly grew to more than 400 subscribers, and requests began to pour in from survivors and caregivers for more frequent words of encouragement, more reassurance, more answers to questions of a spiritual nature, and more advice on how to stay "positive" in the face of a diagnosis of cancer.

It was a big step (and a scary one; could we really come up with something every week?), but we responded with "Weekly Affirmations," little essays and prayers sent out online every Friday.

The response has been overwhelming, to say the least. Our subscriber list is now close to 9,000, and our readers are in every state in the United States and more than 70 countries.

The book you're holding now is a collection of 52 of the most often requested "Weekly Affirmations" and 35 cartoons from "The Cancer Connection."

The Cancer Crusade's mission is to fight cancer with hope and humor. Our greatest wish is that no one ever need take this journey without the friendship and support of others who've been there before them, others who *know*.

We know, and we're here for you.

Kathy & Roger Cawthon
July, 2007

You have been my friend. That in itself is a tremendous thing. I wove my webs for you because I liked you. After all, what's a life anyway? We're born, we live a little while, we die. A spider's life can't help being something of a mess, with all this trapping and eating flies. By helping you, perhaps I was trying to lift up my life a trifle. Heaven knows anyone's life can stand a little of that.

**Charlotte in *Charlotte's Web*
by E.B. White**

Tell me, what is it you plan to do
with your one wild and precious life?

Mary Oliver

Beginning the Journey:

The First 10 Things to Do When the Doctor Says It's Cancer

Grief Work

e must embrace pain and burn it as fuel for our journey. ~ Kenji Miyazawa

A diagnosis of cancer brings us smack into the brick wall of mortality, our own and everyone else's. Confronting this wall – especially if it's for the first time – is huge, the ultimate reality check, and we have to find a way to get beyond it so it doesn't become a permanent barrier to our healing.

No matter how desperately we may wish for a shortcut, the only way to get beyond that wall is to carve out our own passageway and then move right through it. This takes time, and you must give yourself this time. It is absolutely essential to your recovery.

Everyone grieves the loss of perfect health, but not everyone grieves in the same way or for the same length of time. You will know what's right for you. Be extremely gentle with yourself. Care for yourself as if you were your own parent, making sure that you rest and receive nourishment and comfort, but in the ways and at the times that feel right to you.

If others try to redirect your grieving (i.e. by telling you not to cry or to "pull yourself together" or "get a grip" or "put on a smile"), know that they mean well, but also understand that their interference can actually cause you to stumble on your healing journey. The uncomfortable truth is that your grief is upsetting and frightening to them, but *this isn't about them*, so remove yourself from these people and do what you need to do. Find a peaceful place where you can do your work. Grieving is soul work.

A couple of caveats here. The first is for parents of small children. If the intensity of your grieving is such that it could be frightening to them, find a safe place (some churches have retreat houses, many hospitals have weekend retreat programs for seriously ill patients, and the American Cancer Society offers similar retreats for cancer patients) for you to go where you can do your grieving without their having to watch, or allow them to go for a weekend visit with relatives or friends. We did the latter and, while it was not a perfect solution, it was far better than having our children see their mom and dad in the state we were in. They would eventually have to know that both of their parents had been diagnosed with life- threatening cancers, but that bombshell had to wait until we composed ourselves enough to explain it to them in terms they could understand and without unduly frightening them.

One newly diagnosed (and recently widowed) friend of ours was so bombarded by people trying to cheer her up and keep her from crying, and she was so worried about her young daughter witnessing the intensity of her grief that she packed a bag and went to a rented cottage at the beach. Her daughter went to visit her grandmother for the week. It was the off season, and the beach community was practically deserted. Our friend was able to spend several days walking by the ocean, pitching pebbles and shells into the water, alternately shaking her fists and screaming her anger at God, then falling to her knees in the sand, praying and asking Him to embrace and heal her, crying until her tears were all cried out, and finally sleeping around the clock for two days. She returned home, exhausted but relieved, her spirit calm, her courage renewed, a big part of her grief work done. She was ready to face the surgeries and treatments that lay ahead, and she was ready to help her daughter through the difficult days to come.

The second word of caution concerns serious depression. As you move through your grief, it's crucial to communicate with your doctor and let him know how you're handling it. He will want to know that you are moving through the process and not getting "stuck" in your grief. If you do get stuck, he will know what to do to help you get unstuck.

Keep the lines of communication open with both your medical team and your family and friends. Allow those whose presence you find truly comforting to be with you and lend their support, but only on your terms and your schedule. Let them know that you are doing important work and that it is work only you can do, but let them "in" enough that they can be reassured you are okay, that you're moving through your grief and not getting mired in it.

Dear God, watch over me and protect me,
please, as I do my grief work. I'm not myself right now,
and those around me are too frightened to know what's
right for me or them. Guide us through this terrible time,
reminding us that You did not do "this" to us, that
You are grieving with us, and that You are there in the
darkest places and at the scariest times, holding us,
blessing us and healing us with Your love.
~ Amen ~

Courage is being scared to death –
but saddling up anyway.

John Wayne

Breathe

When the breath wanders the mind also is unsteady. But when the breath is calmed the mind too will be still, and (you achieve) long life. Therefore, one should learn to control the breath.

~ Svatmarama

When we panic or remain in a heightened state of anxiety for a period of time, we tend to take rapid, shallow breaths. The longer we breathe this way, the more our panic and anxiety can increase, and we can even experience dizziness and fainting due to hyperventilation.

Become aware of your breathing. Slow it down. Practice deep breathing upon waking in the morning, throughout the day, and at bedtime.

Here is how to begin. Sit quietly and comfortably. Close your eyes. Start by relaxing the muscles of your feet and work your way up your body, relaxing each group of muscles as you go. When you are completely relaxed, focus your attention on your breathing. Breathe in deeply and then let your breath out. Count your breaths, and say the number of the breath as you let it out (this gives you something to do with your mind, helping you to avoid distraction). Do this for ten or twenty minutes. After practicing for a while, slow, deep breathing will become second nature to you, enhancing your mental clarity, helping you conserve your strength, increasing your energy level and helping you sleep better. You will feel calmer and better able to cope with the challenges of your diagnosis and treatments.

There's something else we're talking about, however, when we remind newly diagnosed cancer survivors and those who love them to breathe. We're talking about "taking a breather."

In other words, call a temporary halt to everything if it seems like it's all spinning out of control. Just stop.

The first hours, days and weeks after a cancer diagnosis are frantic for most. You have a million questions. You're frightened. There are so many decisions to make about your family and your work. There is so much to learn. You may have more medical appointments in the next few months than you've had in your entire life. There are treatment decisions that you have to make, decisions that can affect the rest of your life, and you don't even know enough about any of it to *make* any decisions!

This is when you need to stop and take a deep breath, literally and figuratively. *You have time* to learn about your disease, seek second and third opinions, explore treatment options and make decisions. When you feel yourself becoming panicky and your anxiety level shooting through the roof, take a time out. Chances are, nothing has to be decided today.

Talk it over with your doctor. She may tell you that your surgery decision can wait another few days or that your chemotherapy treatments can begin after your vacation or after the holidays. He may tell you a particular medication regimen can wait until after your birthday or your son's wedding or your niece's graduation. The important thing is to discuss it with your doctor and to be open about your concerns and fears. He or she will almost certainly have some solutions and options for you to consider that will have you feeling calmer and more in control right away.

In the meantime, *breathe.*

Dear God, Thank you for giving me the breath of life. Thank you for the air we breathe. Help me to be mindful of every breath I take, inhaling slowly and deeply so that every cell in my body can be enriched and restored by the precious gift of oxygen. As I breathe out, remind me to breathe out also the fear, anger, resentment and other negative emotions that poison my body and spirit. Teach me to breathe, God, so that I might be calm and steady on this difficult journey, and remind me to listen for Your breath as it surrounds me in the wind and the waves and all the rhythms of the earth and sky, that I might be ever mindful of Your presence and protection.

~ Amen ~

**Courage is fear
that has said its prayers.**

Dorothy Bernard

Learn About Your Disease and Know Your Rights

G et up, stand up,
Stand up for your rights.
Get up, stand up,
Never give up the fight.
~ Bob Marley

As a patient, you have important rights, and as we all know, with rights come responsibilities. You have a responsibility to know what your rights are so that you can protect yourself and your loved ones. You will find the "Patient Bill of Rights" below. Study it until you feel confident that you know and understand your rights.

You have other rights, too, simply by virtue of the fact that you are a human being who deserves compassionate care. One of those rights is the right *not* to wait weeks and even months for basic information and compassionate support.

Many patients – if not most – learn that they have cancer from their surgeons, urologists, radiologists, primary care physicians or other medical professionals who are not cancer specialists. As a result, they may initially receive only minimal – if any – information about their diagnoses. The usual process involves the scheduling of yet more tests while patients are sent home to wait...and wait...and wait.

Additional tests and a certain amount of waiting are necessary evils. More tests help further define the diagnosis and provide information that will be helpful in treatment. Unfortunately for the worried patient and his family, these tests and their interpretation take time.

But you don't have to endure that time alone! There are many sources of information and support that you can tap into from the minute you hear the word "cancer."

As soon as you learn that you or a loved one has cancer, request a referral to a medical oncologist (a doctor who specializes in the treatment of cancer). Don't accept an answer of "It's too soon" or "It isn't necessary." We know of cases where referrals have been made even *before* tests confirmed a diagnosis of cancer; compassionate physicians made these referrals in an effort to help calm the patient's fears and make the wait for further results more tolerable. In every case, meeting with an oncologist gave the patient a better understanding of what he was facing and the reassurance that he would be supported and cared for throughout his illness.

If your insurance doesn't accommodate such referrals, ask the diagnosing physician to put you in touch with a patient advocate, social worker and/or other support person who can assist you as you begin to understand your diagnosis.

Take advantage of other resources as well, resources such as the American Cancer Society (800-ACS-2345) and the National Cancer Institute (1-800-4-CANCER). Seek out local support groups (area hospitals and oncology clinics have this information, but you have to ask for it). The best ones are affiliated with major hospitals and cancer treatment centers.

You have the right and the responsibility to learn all you

can about your diagnosis, treatment options and available support services. Remember that *knowledge* is *power*.

Dear God, I bring to You all of my fear and sadness. This news has shaken me so that I don't even know what questions to ask. Please show me the way to move forward. Teach me the questions to ask. Bring me quickly to the people who can answer those questions, who can reassure and comfort me, and who can guide me through this difficult and frightening time. Help me always to remember, God, that You are the Great Physician. I pray for Your healing touch upon my body, my spirit and all of my life.

~ Amen ~

The Patient's Bill of Rights

The following was adopted by the US Advisory Commission on Consumer Protection and Quality in the Health Care Industry in 1998.

Information Disclosure. You have the right to accurate and easily understood information about your health plan, health care professionals, and health care facilities. If you speak another language, have a physical or mental disability, or just don't understand something, assistance will be provided so you can make informed health care decisions.

Choice of Providers and Plans. You have the right to a choice of health care providers that is sufficient to provide you with access to appropriate high-quality health care.

Access to Emergency Services. If you have severe pain, an injury, or sudden illness that convinces you that your health is in serious jeopardy, you have the right to receive screening and stabilization emergency services whenever and wherever needed, without prior authorization or financial penalty.

Participation in Treatment Decisions. You have the right to know your treatment options and to participate in decisions about your care. Parents, guardians, family members, or other individuals that you designate can represent you if you cannot make your own decisions.

Respect and Nondiscrimination. You have a right to considerate, respectful and nondiscriminatory care from your doctors, health plan representatives, and other health care providers.

Confidentiality of Health Information. You have the right to talk in confidence with health care providers and to have your health care information protected. You also have the right to review and copy your own medical record and request that your physician change your record if it is not accurate, relevant, or complete.

Complaints and Appeals. You have the right to a fair, fast, and objective review of any complaint you have against your health plan, doctors, hospitals or other health care personnel. This includes complaints about waiting times, operating hours, the conduct of health care personnel, and the adequacy of health care facilities.

*The only courage that matters
is the kind that gets you from
one moment to the next.*

Mignon McLaughlin

A Fresh Start

*H**ow we spend our days is, of course, how we spend our lives.*   *~ Annie Dillard*

Resolve right now – this minute – to make the positive lifestyle changes you know will improve your chances of a longer, healthier life. Whatever the current status of your health – whether you are a newly diagnosed cancer survivor, long-term survivor, caregiver or have never had any brush with cancer at all – you can absolutely improve the quality of your life and probably extend its length by making some lifestyle changes right now.

The following list of healthy habits is over-simplified, but it's a good start. You can find many excellent books in your local book store and library, and hundreds of websites on the internet, all containing information about what constitutes a healthy lifestyle.

1. Drink water. Everyone needs to drink 6-8 glasses a day, but it is especially important for cancer patients. And drink clean water – bottled or distilled whenever possible.

2. Drink tea. Green or black (the standard varieties and brands found in the grocery store).

3. "Eat the rainbow." Choose most of the foods you eat from plant sources, and eat nine servings of fruits and

vegetables a day. That's right – nine; five is for people who have never had a cancer diagnosis and are not at a particularly high risk. Go heavy on the vegetables. Buy organic produce whenever possible.

4. Cut way back on red meat. Avoid it altogether if you can. Eat fish, or take a daily fish oil supplement if you don't like fish. Occasionally have a little turkey or chicken. As often as possible, eat beans for protein instead of animal products.

5. Get busy. Walk, bike, garden, whatever activity you enjoy and will stick with. Start slow and build up.

6. Maintain a healthy weight. Commit to get there and stay there.

7. While an occasional drink probably isn't harmful and may in fact have some health benefits according to some studies, it's important to talk to your doctor about the use of alcohol during your treatment and recovery periods. This is not the time to start drinking if you don't drink, however, and more than the occasional drink is not good for anyone. You should know that heavy alcohol consumption has been linked to certain types of cancer.

8. Wear sunscreen and, as much as possible, avoid outdoor activities when the sun is at its highest.

9. Avoid vehicle exhaust fumes and the fumes from gasoline when fueling your car or lawn equipment. Choose pest control companies that use organic materials. Avoid exposure to other known carcinogens such as

asbestos, vinyl chloride, chromate and nickel. In fact, avoid chemicals of any kind whenever you can. There is a natural and/or organic substitute for almost every chemical-laden product you are used to using, including cosmetics and toiletries.

10. Get plenty of rest and restful sleep. Talk to your doctor if you are having trouble sleeping or if you sleep but don't feel rested.

Dear God, I thank you again for the amazing gifts of my body and life. Guide me as I strive to unlearn bad habits and replace them with new, healthy ones. Remind me of the simple pleasures of a ripe apple, a cool drink of water, a walk in the sunshine, a nap in the afternoon. Help me learn to be gentle and patient with myself, to give myself time to heal, and to assist my body in its healing by nurturing it with whole, healthy foods, water, exercise and rest.

~ Amen ~

A hero is no braver than an ordinary man, but he is brave five minutes longer.

Ralph Waldo Emerson

*Life is short and we have never
too much time for gladdening the
hearts of those who are traveling the
dark journey with us. Oh, be swift
to love, make haste to be kind.*

Henri Frederick Amiel

Now Is the Time

T he more severe the pain or illness, the more severe will be the necessary changes. These may involve breaking bad habits, or acquiring some new and better ones.   ~ Peter McWilliams

Now is the time to stop doing the things you know you're not supposed to be doing.

You might be amazed at the number of times we have seen cancer patients step outside of treatment centers and light up cigarettes. You might be surprised to learn that many also eat nothing but high-fat fast foods and junk food. You might be dumbfounded to know that some patients show up for surgeries or other treatments under the influence of alcohol and/or illegal drugs. And, believe it or not, some don't show up for their surgeries or treatments at all.

These things might surprise you, and then again they might sound uncomfortably familiar.

Consider this:

If you owned a million-dollar thoroughbred racehorse, would you allow it to be exposed to toxic substances like cigarette smoke? Would you feed it cookies and chips and soda? Would you let it stay out all night, carousing with its horsey friends? Would you give it alcohol or illegal substances? Would you let it skip medical appointments, surgeries or treatments for its health conditions?

Of course not! You'd make sure it breathed clean air, ate only the finest, most nutritious feed, exercised and grazed by day and rested snug in its stall at night, and never ate or drank anything that wasn't beneficial to its overall health and well- being. You'd make sure it had the best medical care available and that it showed up for every appointment, surgery or treatment.

You are not a million-dollar thoroughbred racehorse. You are worth way more than that. You are an *incalculably* precious human being with unlimited potential. Why, oh why, would you do any less for yourself?

If you are doing anything to your body that is negative in any way, that is in any way not healthful and helpful, now is the time to stop.

And while you're working on breaking those bad habits, keep this in mind:

Average cost of a pack of cigarettes or fast food meal: $3.50

Average cost of one chemotherapy treatment: $9000

Your life: ***Priceless***

*Dear God, thank You for my life. Thank You for
my body. Forgive me for not always having cared for
it as I should. Even now, in the midst of this illness,
I sometimes do things that I know are not good for me
and that undermine the work of those who are treating
and caring for me. I pray that You will remove from my
mind, body and spirit the cravings that overpower me.
Replace them with desires to eat healthy foods, drink*

pure water, breathe clean air and exercise every day.
Give me strength, God, to abstain from every action
and inaction detrimental to the priceless body
You have given me.
~ Amen ~

A bit of advice given to a young
Native American at the time of his
initiation: "As you go the way of life,
you will see a great chasm. Jump.
It's not as wide as you think."

Joseph Campbell

"When the doctor said nothing but clear liquids before your colonoscopy, I don't think he meant vodka!"

Avoid
Self-Medicating

A man who treats himself may have a fool for a patient.   ~ Unknown

If you're like many of us, you spend a lot of time online, looking for valid, reliable information about cancer. Because you visit certain websites in your searches, you may find yourself the recipient of e-mail messages touting everything from magical juices to prayers for sale (can you believe it?) that are "guaranteed to cure cancer." Every conceivable "magic bullet" is out there on the web for sale to anyone desperate enough to buy into the pitch.

Please make every effort to report those "cancer cure" messages as spam to your e-mail server, and then make liberal use of the delete key. Whatever you do, *don't buy the products* they want you to buy. The people who promote these products and send these spam messages are the equivalent of the 19th century "snake oil salesmen," people who prey on the ill and frightened in order to make a fast buck.

That's not to say that there aren't some new products on the market that have shown some promise in reducing the risk of certain cancers, and that's not to say that certain vitamins and supplements aren't helpful when taken with full knowledge of what they can and can't do. But we are saying that you need to check with your medical team before trying on your own to boost your cancer treatments.

We're also not talking here about "complementary therapies" such as massage, aromatherapy, exercise, laugh therapy, meditation, yoga, and similar therapies. We encourage cancer survivors – and everyone for that matter – to learn about these techniques and practices and how they can improve your life whether or not you are in treatment for cancer.

But we do want to caution against self-medicating which is very, very different. Many newly diagnosed cancer patients rush to the "natural health and healing" stores and immediately start taking every nutritional supplement and vitamin they can find. *Don't do it.* Talk to your doctor and ask what vitamins and/or supplements – if any – he recommends.

Here's why. Certain supplements, herbal "remedies" and "natural cures" can actually interfere with your medical treatments. For example, St. John's Wort, an all-natural supplement, has been proven in several studies to help some patients with mild-to-moderate depression, *but it has also been found to interfere with the efficacy of several prescription drugs!* And some medical professionals question the safety of soy products by women with certain types of breast cancer, even though soy products have been shown to be beneficial for the general population.

We'd be remiss if we didn't mention self-medicating with alcohol and illegal substances. There's a world of difference between having an occasional drink and drinking yourself into oblivion to try and forget about your next surgery or chemotherapy treatment. Talk to your doctor about the wisdom of having an occasional drink, and never, ever use *any drug* that hasn't been prescribed for you by your doctor.

The bottom line is that only your medical team knows the details of *your* treatment plan and the chemistry of the drugs you are taking and all of the myriad bits of information about *you* and *your* body that need to be taken into consideration before adding anything else to the mix. You may be the captain of the team, but your doctor is the head coach with all the knowledge, skills and experience needed to make important decisions about what goes into *your* body during *your* treatment for cancer. This includes over-the-counter medications, too, such as pain relievers and cold and flu medications.

If there is a certain supplement you want to try, ask the doctor first. Chances are he will say, "Can't hurt. Might help. Go ahead." But far better to be safe than sorry.

Here's the way I look at all of the so-called "miracle cures." Almost every doctor I know (and unfortunately, I know a lot of them) has lost a loved one to cancer. My own oncologist lost his mother. If there were a magic pill or juice or cream or whatever, he certainly would have made sure she received it.

Dear God, so much of what I must endure on this journey is frightening and painful. Sometimes just the knowledge of what the next day will bring is almost more than I can bear. At times like these, it is tempting to look outside the areas of conventional medical wisdom and explore the possibility that there is a simple and painless answer to this disease. Guide me, God, during these times of doubt and weakness. Help me put my faith and trust where it belongs, in the capable hands of the doctors and other medical professionals who treat me, and above all, in You, the Great Physician and Healer who guides those who care for me.

~ Amen ~

"Since my cancer, it's nice to have a doctor standing in **front** of me for a change!"

About That "Positive Attitude" Thing

Everything can be taken from a man but one thing, the last of the human freedoms – to choose one's attitude in any given set of circumstances, to choose one's own way.

~ Viktor Frankl

I don't know about you, but I got to where I hated hearing that "positive attitude" thing. Especially from people who had never faced cancer. Not only did I get tired of hearing it – mainly because everyone was so sure I *needed* a positive attitude, but no one could tell me how to *get* one – but it also frightened me. It usually came with a knowing look and the assertion that I would never be able to beat my disease without the "PA." And so, I reasoned, since I didn't *have* one at the time, that must mean I didn't have a snowball's chance in Miami.

What I didn't know then and would need several years to learn (but you won't because now you have the benefit of my sad experience!) is that a positive attitude about something as devastating as a cancer diagnosis takes time. In some cases, lots of time. And that I needed to be very gentle and patient with myself. And that it was okay to be angry and sad and scared and that, in fact, it was healthy to fully experience and work through whatever emotions I felt because – *and this is very, very important* – there's no room for the good stuff until you get rid of the bad stuff.

So stop being hard on yourself if you're just not there yet. Work through the grief and the anger and the fear. It is not – *repeat: NOT* – going to hurt you. It can only help because it brings you that much closer to being ready to work on cultivating a positive attitude (more about that in a minute). So cry, beat the bed with a tennis racket, throw rocks in the ocean or eggs in the sink, talk it over with a therapist or spiritual advisor, sit in your car with the windows up and scream, whatever it takes. Think of it as opening up and cleaning out an infected wound. You have to do the painful work before the healing can begin.

When you've done that work, you can begin to cultivate a positive attitude. Here are some suggestions.

Don't look for or listen to statistics and "time limits." The fact is that somebody has beaten every kind of cancer there is. There are survivors of every type and stage of this disease. No one – not even your doctor – has all the answers or can tell you with 100% certainty what the outcome of your diagnosis and treatment will be. The best anyone can do is venture an educated guess based on statistical probabilities, and no matter what their best guess is, it isn't going to do you one bit of good, so best to just leave it alone. You have far more important things to do, so go forth and do these things.

Stay connected to friends and family. They're struggling with your diagnosis, too. Allow them to care for you. Giving and receiving care are healing for the giver and the receiver. On the other hand, if you find that certain people can only be negative around you and want to tell you about Great Aunt

Flo who died *"of the very same thing"* (without bothering to mention, of course, that she died thirty years ago when there were fewer effective treatments; also remember that no one has ever had *"the very same thing"* you have because no two cases are alike – *ever*), avoid them, at least for the time being. With friends like that, who needs an enema? (Sorry. I love that joke.)

This next one may seem a little far out, but stay with me here. ***Wear clothes that make you feel braver and stronger or that just make you feel good or that make you and those around you laugh.*** I discovered this one by accident one day when I had to grab one of my son's "No Fear" shirts to wear to the treatment center because I hadn't done the laundry; when I walked in, several people noted the slogan on the shirt, gave me a big thumbs-up and said things like "That's the spirit!" That got me thinking, and so I began to ally myself with the Army, the Marine Corps, a local fire department and the regional police academy by wearing their t-shirts. I found that those shirts made me feel like part of a team of strong, powerful people. I adopted a "warrior mentality" and began to carry that image of myself in my head: me as a soldier fighting for my life – *and winning.* I also made sure I wore bright colors, and sometimes I wore shirts and hats that were funny so I could make others laugh. I found that what I wore had a powerful effect on my mood and sometimes even the moods of others.

On good days, I put on make-up and either styled my wig or wore a pretty turban, and I put on colorful, pretty clothes. On bad days, this was a challenge, and on *really* bad days, I didn't worry about my appearance at all. Sometimes just focusing on getting through the day is all you can handle, and that's fine. Again, be gentle with yourself. If worrying about the way you look only adds to your fatigue and discomfort, *forget about it!* This is your party – although admittedly a *really* lousy party – and you get to determine the dress code.

Create and practice comforting rituals. At times of crisis and upheaval in our lives, it helps to stick to familiar routines as much as possible. Additionally, we can find even more comfort by including soothing rituals in our daily schedules. Set aside time to brew a pot of tea, soak in a warm bath, rest while listening to a CD of a rain shower or ocean waves, light a candle and meditate or pray. Rituals are calming and restorative. Create your own and make them a part of your daily healing.

Celebrate every milestone. Stitches out today? Celebrate! Last chemotherapy or radiation treatment? Celebrate! First hair growing back? For gosh sakes, *celebrate!* Whatever your favorite *healthy* means of celebrating, do it. Go out to dinner. Buy yourself a special gift. Go away for the weekend. Have friends over. Do it up big or keep it small, but celebrate every step along your journey of healing.

Remember that humor heals. Go to the website of the American Film Institute (www.afi.com) and follow the links to their listing of the 100 funniest movies ever made. Then head for the video store (or send someone else if you're not up to it) and start working your way through the list. Watch, read and listen to funny tapes, books and CDs. Watch sitcoms and those "funniest videos" specials on TV. Likewise, avoid scary, sad or violent movies and books. Not only are you what you eat; you are also what you read and observe.

Utilize positive visualizations. Put in a tape or CD of healing music or nature sounds, and do some deep breathing to bring yourself into a calm, relaxed state. With your eyes closed and your breathing slow and steady, create a mental picture of yourself as a strong, healthy survivor. Take that image through whatever experience represents for you the achievement of your goal. See yourself strong and well, robust and healthy, a long-term cancer survivor enjoying life to the fullest, engaged in activities you enjoy, surrounded by loved ones, laughing and joyful. Be sure to visit the "Meditation Room" on our website for free, downloadable meditations (www.TheCancerCrusade.com).

Savor pleasurable things. Be fully aware and mindful – *be in the moment* – when you are engaged in an activity that gives you pleasure. Eating the first strawberry or the last watermelon in summer or the first apple of fall. Watching a storm or a sunset. Dancing with someone you love. Reading a novel. Building a model ship. Whatever gives you pleasure – as long as it doesn't interfere with or compromise your treatment – do it and *savor every moment!*

Dear God, give me patience as I work through the grief, anger and fear that come with a diagnosis of cancer. Help me release these dark emotions and bring me once again into Your light. Show me how to be positive, Lord, while facing this disease and the pain and uncertainty it has brought into my life. Show me the way back to health and joy, back to myself and back to You.

~ Amen ~

47

One isn't necessarily born with courage, but one is born with potential. Without courage, we cannot practice any other virtue with consistency. We can't be kind, true, merciful, generous, or honest.

Maya Angelou

Keep a Journal

I became a writer out of desperation...When I was young, younger than I am now, I started to write about my own life and I came to see that this act saved my life.   ~ Jamaica Kincaid

You are at a crossroads in your life's journey and, whether you realize it now or not, you are growing and changing into a different person – a better person in many ways – than the person you were before your diagnosis. The day will come when you will want to look back over this experience and marvel at all you have learned from it and even the many blessings you received as a result. Keeping a journal now will help you recall circumstances, events, people and details that your memory simply will not retain.

Keeping a journal will also help you remember questions you want to ask your doctor, symptoms and treatment side effects that were here one day and gone the next that you need to discuss with her. It will also give you a visual readout of your good days and bad days so that you have a better idea when one or the other is coming and can be prepared for it.

But most of all, it's important to keep a journal because it can be a healing activity. Journaling is an opportunity to examine your experiences, to process them thoughtfully and to find greater meaning in them. An experience examined becomes richer, deeper, more powerful.

Journaling is also cathartic. You can rant in your journal, rage at the insensitivity of others to your condition, scream at the tedious and painful treatments, curse the night, spill your darkest fears, bleed through your pen onto the paper. Get the bad stuff out to make way for the good stuff. As singer/songwriter Joni Mitchell said, "The most important thing is to write in your own blood" (but please don't take that literally!).

As a final step in each journal entry, record joy. You will have to look harder for joy on some days than on others, but if you look hard enough, you will find it. Write about a person you encountered who smiled or said something kind or supported you in some way and made you feel better. Write about something you did well. Write about something you like about yourself.

If today is just too sad and difficult, recall a joyful time in your past. Write about activities you enjoyed as a child, and think and write about ways you could enjoy them again when you're feeling better.

Write about your partner and the things you adore about him or her. Write about what it felt like when you fell in love. Write about times when you've felt peaceful and serene, strong and powerful, silly and downright giddy. Write about a time you laughed so hard you cried or milk came out of your nose.

Write about someone you need to forgive. Write a thank-you note to God. Count your blessings, and write them down.

Dear God, I am beginning to understand that the anger, fear and sadness I carry around with me can be harmful to my body, mind and spirit if I don't find healthy ways to release them. Show me these ways, Lord, and guide me to the ones that are right for me. I'm also beginning to understand that making a conscious effort to find joy in every day can help me along the path of healing. Today I am struggling with this, and I pray that you will turn my soul in the direction of joy and open my eyes and spirit to receive it.

~ Amen ~

Yesterday I dared to struggle.

Today I dare to win.

Bernadette Devlin

Finding Your Spiritual Self

I have one life and one chance to make it count for something... I'm free to choose what that something is, and the something I've chosen is my faith. Now, my faith goes beyond theology and religion and requires considerable work and effort. My faith demands – this is not optional – my faith demands that I do whatever I can, wherever I am, whenever I can, for as long as I can with whatever I have to try to make a difference.

~ President Jimmy Carter

The spiritual journey is, of course, a very personal one. You may have been raised in a family that had strong religious ties to one faith, or you may have grown up in an environment where there was little or no emphasis on religion. Whatever your spiritual or religious background and beliefs, now is the time to explore and practice them, even if you haven't given them a thought in years.

If you've never given much thought to your spiritual or religious beliefs or if you're no longer comfortable with the ones you grew up with, this can be an exciting time of exploration and discovery.

You may want to meet with a pastor, priest, rabbi, shaman or other leader/counselor from your own faith or culture or one you want to learn more about. Or you may prefer to embark upon a spiritual quest on your own. A good place to begin is at your local book store or library where you will find hundreds of books about many faith traditions from all over the world as well as books about the broader subject of spirituality.

You may recall religious rituals that brought you comfort in the past, lighting a candle in a chapel or singing a favorite hymn or chanting a prayer or blessing. Or you may want to try these things for the first time. Whether you choose to worship in a formal setting or connect with your Higher Power privately in a place that has special meaning for you, find a way to make that connection, and then make it a part of your everyday life.

Cancer patients who have strong ties to religious and cultural traditions move more easily through their diagnoses and treatments and feel more supported and hopeful overall.

When you're ready – and believe me, that day will come – remember that, as a cancer survivor, you have an enormous opportunity to care for and comfort others who have received a diagnosis of cancer. At that time, you can live your faith and be a shining example of the power of the spirit by encouraging them to embark on their own journeys of spiritual discovery.

Prayer of St. Francis of Assisi

Lord, make me an instrument of Your peace.
Where there is hatred, let me sow love;
*   where there is injury,pardon;*
*   where there is doubt, faith;*
*   where there is despair, hope;*
*   where there is darkness, light;*
*   and where there is sadness, joy.*
O Divine Master, grant that I may not
*   so much seek to be consoled as to console;*
*   to be understood as to understand;*
*   to be loved as to love.*
For it is in giving that we receive;
*   it is in pardoning that we are pardoned;*
*   and it is in dying that we are born to eternal life.*

~ Amen ~

Only when we are no longer afraid
do we begin to live.

Dorothy Thompson

Be Amazing

*T*wenty years from now you will be more disappointed by the things you didn't do than by the ones you did do. So throw off the bowlines. Sail away from the safe harbor. Catch the trade winds in your sails. Explore. Dream. Discover.

~ Mark Twain

A friend of mine and fellow cancer survivor arrived flushed and breathless at a recent gathering and pulled me aside. "You'll never believe what I did!" she exclaimed, taking my hands in hers. I'd never seen her looking so radiant or so joyful in the five years she had been battling breast cancer. The freckles were practically popping off her beautiful face.

"I went skydiving," she said, her eyes wild with excitement. "I did it! I jumped out of an airplane!"

She went on to explain that she had gotten the idea from the popular song by Tim McGraw, "Live Like You Were Dying." She had contacted a local skydiving club and learned that they had regular jump days for people with no experience. After a few hours of instruction and practice, each person who had registered made the jump in tandem with an instructor. By the time my friend finished describing the exhilaration she had experienced that day *and the overwhelming sense of triumph and victory she had gained from it*, I was almost ready to strap on a parachute.

Every cancer survivor should plan to *do something amazing*. And, no, it certainly does not have to be something like skydiving! That was the right thing for my friend, but it wasn't the right thing for me after all (it turns out that freefalling and motion sickness are not a good combination). I've done other things since my cancer diagnosis that amazed those around me, but the most important person I amazed was myself. And that's what we want to encourage you to do.

Those of us who have had a diagnosis of cancer have a unique opportunity to grasp some real life truths that many others leave this world without ever understanding: that our mortality is a gift (if human beings lived forever, our days would have no meaning), and that even the youngest, healthiest, strongest person among us is not guaranteed tomorrow. We all need to forget about how much time we may or may not have, because *nobody* knows. We need to pick up right where we are today and *do something amazing* with whatever time we have left.

You've had fantasies. You know you have! Have you secretly wished you had become an actor or a musician or an artist? Have you harbored a desire to study pharmacy or criminal justice or the culture of a primitive population? Ever thought of taking a photographic safari? Climbing a mountain? White water rafting? Learning shorthand? Building a birdhouse, a garage, a website? Do you love to experiment in the kitchen? The lab? The garden? Want to write a book? Produce a play? Compose a musical score? Have you always wished you'd learned to play tennis? Swim? Ice skate?

We could ask hundreds of these questions, but you get the picture. Examine those fantasies and pick one. Write out your plans. Take baby steps. The acting thing? Try out for a play with a local theatre troupe. The musician thing? Buy a recorder and a teach-yourself-to-play book. A photographic safari? Spend an afternoon in the backyard with a simple camera. Wish you had become an artist? Pick up a pencil and some paper and start drawing. Baby steps. You get the idea.

And while you may be in treatment today and not up to climbing that mountain or putting on a pair of skates, that doesn't mean you won't be up to it in a few months or next year. So go to the library or bookstore today – or send a friend – to get some books for you on the subject of your heart's desire. Rent a video that shows people doing what you want to do. Read about it. Write about it. Dream about it. Close your eyes and visualize yourself doing it.

Live it, if only in your imagination for right now.

You are amazing! Show yourself and the world the amazing stuff you're made of.

Dear God, I'm not feeling so amazing right now.
I'm not sure I ever will again. But I know You put me
on this earth for a reason and that my life has meaning.
You gave me gifts and talents, and You breathed life into
me so that I might use those gifts and talents to return
something amazing to You. Show me how to do that, Lord.
Breathe new life into my days and remind me of the
dreams that once burned inside me. Teach me one tiny
thing today, God. Guide me as I learn to dream again,
to remember that I am amazing and to believe that
I can do amazing things.
~ Amen ~

Courageous risks are life-giving;
they help you grow, make you brave, and
better than you think you are.

Joan L. Curcio

Becoming a Survivor

Who and What Is "A Survivor"?

I f children have the ability to ignore all odds and percentages, then maybe we can all learn from them. When you think about it, what other choice is there but to hope? We have two options, medically and emotionally: give up, or fight like hell.

~ Lance Armstrong

How do you define a survivor? We've heard responses ranging from "You are a survivor from the instant a tumor begins to form" to "You are a survivor as soon as all of your treatments are over" to "You are a survivor as soon as the tumor is surgically removed."

While these definitions may serve for some, they are not broad enough to include all cancer survivors because they assume all cancers are the same in that there is a tumor (sometimes there isn't), in that there is surgery (sometimes there isn't), and that there is a finite number of treatments for every patient (sometimes there isn't). These definitions also assume that there is a set point, a certain number of years out from diagnosis at which a person can begin to call himself a survivor, but that doesn't work either because some cancers have a low risk of recurrence and are considered beaten after a certain number of years while other cancers have a high risk of recurrence and are never considered beaten. Even though we were diagnosed at the same time eleven years ago, can Roger call himself a survivor now because his type of cancer has a low recurrence rate, but I cannot because my type of cancer can recur many years later? What would the magic number of years be? The answer is, of course, that there is no magic number.

Many people don't like the word "survivor" for a variety of reasons, most of which reflect a great deal of anger, anxiety and fear.

We would like to offer another – and, we believe, infinitely healthier – way of interpreting the word "survivor."

Our favorite response – and the definition to which we at The Cancer Crusade adhere – is that "You become a survivor the moment you learn your diagnosis and make up your mind to fight."

The word "survivor" is about being a warrior, a fighter who is going to go the distance and do whatever it takes to give himself the best odds of beating his disease. Think about it. Being a survivor is an attitude, a state of mind.

If achieving this attitude is difficult for you, try using a technique called "creative visualization" to help yourself achieve this state of mind. Take a few minutes to breathe deeply and focus on relaxing all the muscles of your body. Then close your eyes and form a mental picture of yourself clothed in armor, chest out, head held high, ready to march into battle. Hold the image for as long as you can, but for at least 3-5 minutes. As you practice this technique, watch your warrior-self actually go into battle against your disease and defeat your disease every time. Practice this visualization at least twice a day, working your way up to holding the image for at least 10 minutes. Don't worry or get frustrated if your mind wanders or the image gets fuzzy. Just gently bring the image back to mind and hold it for as long as you can.

Be a fighter. Have a warrior mentality. That's what we believe defines a survivor.

Think about this, too. If you don't like to be called a survivor, what are the options? Patient? Invalid? Victim? We don't know about you, but we'll take "survivor" any day.

Dear God, thank You for giving me the opportunity to fight my disease. I ask now for courage to face the challenges each day brings and endurance to go the distance. Bless my battle, Lord, and protect me. Help me stay focused on recovery, not illness, so that I may rise up strong in the days to come. Fill every cell of my being with Your light and love.

~ Amen ~

The best way out is always through.

Robert Frost

*Character cannot be developed
in ease and quiet. Only through
experiences of trial and suffering
can the soul be strengthened,
vision cleared, ambition inspired,
and success achieved.*

Helen Keller

Am I a Survivor?

*J*ust when the caterpillar thought the world had ended, it became a butterfly. ~ Unknown

A reader recently wrote the following: "Since my surgery (mastectomy) and subsequent reconstruction, two of my friends had mastectomies. However, my friends needed radiation and chemotherapy, and they suffered all that those treatments have to offer...I always feel incredibly guilty when I see these women (and those like them) who have undergone so much more than I have. I don't feel the right to call myself a survivor when, in fact, my battle pales by comparison. Have you ever come across this problem?"

Her question reminded me of other survivors I know. A friend of ours refuses to walk the "Survivors Lap" at our local Relay For Life because she says she "only" had a small skin cancer removed from her arm. Another says she doesn't feel like she has the right to call herself a survivor because she "only" had a lumpectomy and 33 radiation treatments. And yet another says that he's not sure he's a "real" survivor because he "only" had part of one lung removed while a friend of his had surgery, chemotherapy and radiation treatments.

Children who have a certain type of leukemia often undergo more than two years of chemotherapy. We know a woman who has been living with cancer for 14 years and has undergone months and months of chemotherapy and other treatments more a dozen times. My own mother recently completed 35 radiation treatments for breast cancer, and my step-father was recently diagnosed with prostate cancer and will undergo a surgical implantation of radiation "seeds." My best friend had a mastectomy with reconstruction, chemotherapy and radiation treatments.

The simple fact is that, with a disease as complex as cancer (and remember that there are more than 100 types of cancer), the possible treatment variations and combinations are infinite! Also, suffering is subjective. What I think is painful, you might find merely uncomfortable. What you find intolerable, I might think is little more than annoying. If we were to require a certain type or number of surgeries and/ or treatments in order to be considered survivors, or if we were to engage in questioning how much or how little one has "suffered," what would be the magic number or degree, extent or level of intensity? The answer is, of course, that we cannot go there. It's a pointless exercise and a waste of time and energy, and I don't know about you, but I don't have any of either to spare!

If you have had a doctor tell you "You have cancer," you have suffered a psychological blow like no other. You have experienced an emotional trauma that no one who has not had cancer can comprehend. For me, being given the diagnosis was the very worst of the entire cancer experience. When I look back on my surgeries, chemotherapy and radiation treatments, I am acutely aware that – while they certainly were no picnic – they were not nearly as awful as the day my doctor told me I had cancer.

If you survived that day in your own life, you are a survivor, because being a survivor is not about how many or what kind of treatments we have. In fact, it has nothing at all to do with our bodies. It's about how big our spirits are and how we carry ourselves in the face of fear and danger. It's about grace and dignity and courage and heart.

Dear God, please help me remember to celebrate myself,
to look back on how far I've come and all that I've
endured and achieved along this difficult journey, even
if it just began yesterday. Remind me that it's okay to
be proud of who and what and where I am today.
No matter how my story ends, I am a survivor.
~ Amen ~

Never let the fear of striking out
get in your way.

Babe Ruth

69

Life is the only real counselor;
wisdom unfiltered through personal
experience does not become a part
of the moral tissue.

Edith Wharton

Developing a
Warrior Mentality

*T*he basic difference between an ordinary man
and a warrior is that a warrior takes everything
as a challenge while an ordinary man takes
everything either as a blessing or a curse.

~ Carlos Casteneda

Begin today to transform yourself into a warrior. No, you don't have to go on any training runs or scale 8-foot obstacles or crawl through the mud with bullets flying around your head (although if you're currently in treatment, you may feel like you've done all those things at the ends of some days!).

No, what we want you to start doing today is thinking about the brave young men and women who defend our country and put their lives on the line every day for total strangers around the world and how they go about preparing for war. We will take our lessons from them.

The first thing warriors do is study the enemy. They learn all that they can about the enemy, especially his weaknesses. They know that knowledge is power, and they arm themselves with as much intelligence as can be gathered.

As General Patton taught us when he studied the battle strategies of Napoleon, warriors study known and proven tactics. Those basic tactics and strategies always provide the foundation of the battle plans, even though many improvements and additions have been made in the years since their development.

Warriors gather the best weapons available to them and then clean and oil those weapons. A soldier knows that his weapon is his best friend.

A warrior trains constantly, both physically and mentally. He focuses on good nutrition and staying hydrated at all times.

A warrior maintains a positive attitude and focus at all times. He keeps his eyes on the victory to come.

Warriors gather a coalition of allies. They surround themselves with the strongest, bravest, most intelligent comrades-in-arms, and they bond tightly to one another.

And when they have done all that they can humanly do to prepare for battle, warriors seek divine guidance. They humbly pray for protection, safety, leadership, miracles and victory.

As survivors and caregivers facing cancer, how can we do any less? Each of us *must* develop a warrior mentality.

1. **Study the enemy** (learn about your disease and what its weaknesses are) **and the known and proven tactics** (treatments and changes in lifestyle) that have stopped its advance, brought it under control or defeated it in the past.

2. **Gather your weapons.** Line up and schedule whatever tests and treatments your treatment team has recommended, and then show up for them; ask about clinical trials and insist on the best, most cutting-edge treatments available; travel if necessary.

3. **Train physically and mentally every day.** You may not be able to run or do sit-ups, but you can move around your house or even your bedroom or even just in your bed! Do whatever you can to stretch your muscles, get your blood circulating – power up! Eat only the finest, freshest foods available (eat a mostly plant-based diet, organic whenever possible). Drink water until your urine runs clear. Then meditate, practice deep breathing, calm yourself with soft music, recorded nature sounds, meditation tapes or CDs. Close your eyes and visualize victory. Do this as many times a day as you possibly can. Fall asleep each night with your "victory vision" clearly in mind.

4. **Maintain a positive focus at all times.** Yes, I know, there will be days when this seems impossible, but be a warrior! Bring your focus back to where it's supposed to be. Keep your eyes on the prize. See only victory.

5. **Gather a coalition of allies.** Put your treatment in the hands of medical professionals you trust, *and then trust them*! Surround yourself with friends and family members who will help you maintain your positive focus. Have one family member or friend who can "run interference" for you by asking anyone who can't be positive around you not to call or visit for the time being. Place yourself in the middle of a circle of healers and loved ones. Close your eyes often and visualize yourself in the middle of this powerful, protective circle.

6. And when you have done all that you can humanly do to prepare for battle, **seek divine guidance**. Pray for protection and safety, pray for strength and courage, pray for miracles and pray for victory.

The Cancer Warrior's Prayer
(based on The Marine Prayer)

Almighty Father, whose command is over all and whose love never fails, make me aware of Thy presence and obedient to Thy will. Keep me true to my best self, guarding and helping me to live so that I can face myself, my loved ones and Thee without self-pity or fear. Give me the will to do the healing work of a cancer warrior and to accept my treatments with confidence and resolve. Grant me the courage to accept the challenges of each day. If I am inclined to doubt, steady my faith; if I am tempted to surrender, make me strong to resist. Guide me with the light of truth and grant me wisdom by which I may understand the answers to my prayers.
~ Amen ~

Cancer makes a woman out of you.
After that you become a warrior.
Survival is not so much about the
body, but rather it is about the
triumph of the human spirit.

Danita Vance

"The doctor said this might cause me to have a thrombotic event, but I told him not to worry. I went to one of those in college, and I was fine!"

Embrace
the Dragon

*Y*ou gain strength, courage, and confidence by every experience in which you really stop to look fear in the face. You must do the thing which you think you cannot do.   ~ Eleanor Roosevelt

According to legend, Shaolin temple monks had to endure an agonizing test of endurance and courage in order to achieve the level of master. They were made to strip naked and embrace a branding vessel that had been emblazoned with an image of a dragon. The resulting "dragon scar" was proof that the monk could face and overcome his fears.

Many people refer to cancer as "the beast," and being diagnosed is often compared to "facing the dragon." Cancer is indeed a terrifying diagnosis to receive, and it is little wonder that the first instinct for many of us is to turn away, to say *I can't do this*, to be paralyzed by fear.

But consider for a moment whether we might do better to consciously employ a different technique, that of embracing the dragon, and whether by doing so, we might be more successful in taming the beast and finally defeating it.

One of the earliest stories in which someone who is threatened by a dragon makes use of this technique is the story of St. George. George, (not a saint yet, of course, but just a tribune in the Roman army) came across a maiden

77

who was being held captive by a dragon. The dragon was hiding nearby (they're sneaky that way), and the maiden – quite understandably – was weeping. When George asked her why she was crying, she urged him to "quickly mount your horse and fly less you perish with me."

Of course, the brave tribune stood his ground and asked of what she was so afraid. Just then, the dragon emerged from its hiding place and the maiden screamed (maidens did a lot of that back then). George, however, made the sign of the cross, uttered a brief prayer (it is often necessary to be brief when facing dragons), and advanced on the dragon. Brandishing his lance (don't worry; you won't need one of these), he transfixed the beast and cast it to the ground. He instructed the maiden to pass her girdle (I don't think "girdle" meant the same thing in those days) around the dragon – *note that she "embraced" the dragon!* – and to fear nothing. When this had been done, the dragon followed her like a puppy!

George and the maiden then led the dragon into the town it had been terrorizing. The people fled, but George called them back and told them they no longer needed to fear the dragon because he had been sent to deliver them. After much celebrating and baptizing, George smote off the head of the dragon.

While we as cancer survivors are not required to face down a fiery dragon (and I for one am *very* thankful for that!) or do any actual smoting (again, *grateful!*), we can learn a powerful lesson from the Shaolin temple monks and St. George. By turning and facing "the beast" head on, showing no fear even when your knees are knocking and your heart is pounding, and maybe even shouting "Bring it on!" above the dragon's roar, we can tame it enough to embrace it, not with affection, mind you, but in an act of absolute power and control.

In yet another bit of dragon lore, it is said that by embracing a dragon, you absorb a bit of its heart and its courage. And who among us couldn't use a little more of that?

Dear God, I find that I must face the beast called "cancer," and I am more afraid than I have ever been. I can and will stand up to this enemy, Lord, because I know that You are behind me as I move forward into this fight, and if I fall, it will be into Your arms. I know, too, that You are in front of me as my shield and beside me as my sword. Whatever the outcome, I will prevail because You are mightier than any evil or hurtful thing, and because I am Yours.
~ Amen ~

We must face what we fear; that is the case of the core of the restoration of health.

Max Lerner

Strength does not come from winning.
Your struggles develop your strengths.
When you go through hardships
and decide not to surrender,
that is strength.

Arnold Schwarzenegger

Fighting Back

The race belongs not only to the swift and the strong, but also to those who keep running.

~ Unknown

We weren't trying to fool anybody. Neither of us was what you would call even remotely athletic when we decided to enter the Marine Corps Marathon. Neither of us had exercised in years, we were overweight, and – as one of our doctors so diplomatically put it – we weren't exactly "spring chickens" anymore.

Not to mention we had both just come through the most harrowing time of our lives, Roger having lost a kidney to cancer and my having had nearly a year of aggressive treatment for breast cancer.

I think what fueled our decision to run a marathon was some residual anger. We were angry at ourselves for not having kept in better shape for the last twenty-five years. We were angry that we had ignored all of the wonderful advice on staying healthy that is around all of us all the time. We were angry that cancer had invaded our lives and threatened to take them from us. We were angry that our children were terrified and other family members and friends felt helpless and scared for us.

We wanted and needed to fight back somehow, to prove to ourselves that we could and would find meaning in what had happened to us. Most of all, we wanted to shore up our bodies and our spirits in hopes of keeping a recurrence or new diagnosis at bay.

So we made the decision to run a marathon. (By the way and for the record, we use the term "run" very loosely. We would ultimately hobble, stumble and limp our way to the finish line. Our only goal was to finish the same day we started!)

As we began to train and talk about our plan, we were stunned by the reactions from quite a few folks in the athletic community. We joined a local fitness center and a regional track club where we met many people who insisted often and not too subtly that a marathon was out of the question for people like us. Some very serious competitive runners were even hostile toward us! They were angry that "charity runners" like us (our marathon entry was guaranteed and sponsored by a foundation for which we had raised funds) take up marathon spaces they felt should be reserved for "serious runners."

We didn't understand how what we were doing could have been any more "serious." We were literally running for our lives, not a prize purse or trophy or even a finisher's medal. Completing this marathon had, for us, become symbolic of our triumph over the fear and sorrow of cancer. It was our way of fighting back and beginning to develop what we would later come to refer to as a "warrior mentality."

Whatever you decide to take on as your personal battle plan against cancer – whether it be a marathon, a fundraising drive, writing your memoirs, going back to school or a new business (the possibilities are endless!) – don't let the naysayers discourage you. The race belongs to everyone because it is about being alive right now, today, this minute, and celebrating every moment.

*Dear God, strengthen my resolve and courage today
as I struggle to overcome my limitations and to ignore
those who focus only on what they think I can't or
shouldn't do. I pray that you bring into my life people
who believe in me and who help me believe in myself
and my ability to fight my illness any way I choose.*
~ Amen ~

**You don't get to choose how
you're going to die. Or when.
You can only decide how you're
going to live. Now.**

Joan Baez

Scars

Your scars are beautiful. They are the brushstrokes in the masterpiece that is your life.

~ Kathy Cawthon

Ancient legend tells of the powerful Amazons, a race of one-breasted female warriors. These fierce fighting women, known for their skill as archers, underwent voluntary mastectomies so their breasts would not interfere with their aim. Their very survival depended upon the radical surgery.

Legend also tells of the Scythian culture in which women were expected to fight alongside the men. A mastectomy of the right breast was performed on female infants to prevent weakening of the pectoral muscle on that side. This ensured the girls would be able to brandish a sword with power and skill.

Scholars debate whether there is any truth behind these popular stories, but – true or not – the tales provide us with a thought-provoking way in which to reframe the ways in which we view our scars.

Instead of looking at the scars on our bodies as reminders of illness and weakness, we could look at them as evidence that illness and weakness were *removed* from our bodies, making us more powerful than we were before. We could take pride in our scars because they are proof of battles we have fought and won. They speak of our courage and resolve.

They tell the stories of our lives.

As we age, our faces and bodies naturally develop lines and wrinkles in addition to the scars that result from accidents and surgeries. Instead of fighting the lines and wrinkles with cosmetic surgeries and hiding our battle scars as if they are shameful or embarrassing, why not look at them as evidence of the rich collection of experiences that have shaped our characters over time and made us who we are today?

Each of us is a miracle, and each of us is a masterpiece of the Creator. One-of-a-kind. No two alike. A singular work of art full of power and promise.

Rejoice in all of your brushstrokes!

Heavenly Father, help me to remember that I am Your creation and that everything You have created is perfect and beautiful.
~ Amen ~

Life is just a chance to grow a soul.

A. Powell Davies

There remain times when one can only endure. One lives on, one doesn't die, and the only thing that one can do is to fill one's mind and time as far as possible with the concerns of other people. It doesn't bring immediate peace, but it brings the dawn nearer.

Arthur Christopher Benson

A Practical Guide to Fighting Fear

W hen I hear music, I fear no danger. I am invulnerable. I see no foe. I am related to the earliest times, and to the latest.

~ Henry David Thoreau

I am often asked by both survivors of cancer and those who have never experienced that awful diagnosis, "Aren't you scared it will come back?" Well, yeah, as a matter of fact I am. I don't know anyone who has ever had cancer who doesn't worry about a recurrence. My anxiety becomes especially acute when it's time to see my oncologist for blood work and other tests.

While I have not had a recurrence, I have many, many friends who have, and they also battle fear on a daily basis – fears of new treatments and unpredictable side effects, and the overwhelming fear of the unknown which is where all cancer survivors begin their journeys.

Thankfully, I've learned from my fellow "survivor warriors" some ways to fight the fear and to keep it from preventing my enjoyment of life, and I'd like to share some of them with you.

Simply put, I fight fear by constantly trying new things, exploring new healing activities and ideas. For example, I recently attended a therapeutic drumming workshop sponsored by a local hospital. The workshop facilitator brought about 30 drums from all over the world. After inviting each of us to select a drum, she began teaching us simple rhythms and songs, and by the end of the 2-hour workshop, we were drumming and singing like pros! Well, okay, maybe not pros, but you'd have been amazed at how great we sounded! We certainly were!

She led us in a drumming prayer-song at the end of the session. We prayed for our own healing and the healing of hurting people everywhere, and we prayed for the healing of our world. At the end of the evening, I knew I had had a powerful spiritual experience. I also felt more aerobically energized than I have even after a strenuous workout. I slept better that night than I have in years. I'm now shopping for my first drum, and I'm also looking at Native American flutes and thinking I would like to learn to play that beautiful instrument. See what I mean? I try always to be open to learning new things (new to me, anyway) and accepting new challenges because I know they can and will absorb the negative energy of my fears before those fears can affect my physical health and my emotional well-being.

By the way, you don't have to have access to a therapeutic drumming workshop or any of the other suggested activities here. Drums and other instruments are available at a wide variety of websites, and you can find CDs to drum along with as well as instructional CDs and anything else you need to start your own one-man band!

Other fear-fighting activities I find extremely helpful include using a hand-held labyrinth for prayer and meditation, simple yoga exercises (using a DVD), deep breathing and meditation using various CDs of soothing music and nature sounds, walking, drawing and painting, and writing.

I find that creative kinds of "busy" are the best at carrying us away from fearful thoughts and worries. "Creative" doesn't have to translate to "arts and crafts." Everyone can create something – a melody, a recipe, a collage, a photograph. The possibilities are limited only by your own imagination.

I recall hearing or reading somewhere that "there are only two forces in the universe: one is fear, and the other is love. When you stand on one, the other cannot touch you." When I begin to feel fearful, I remind myself to "stand on love."

Great Creator, help me remember that we were all created by You in Your image, and that means we are creative beings by our very nature. You have called us to be creators and to create from the vast supply of materials You have given us. Guide me to create so that I may leave beauty, passion, joy and love along the pathway of my life's journey.

~ Amen ~

I am not afraid of tomorrow, for I have seen yesterday and I love today.

William Allen White

Overcoming Cancer Guilt

*T**he past cannot be changed. The future is yet in your power.*   ~ Hugh White*

Shortly after my breast cancer diagnosis, I read a newspaper article that quoted a study on risk factors for breast cancer. The results indicated that women who had participated in track and field events in high school had a lower risk of breast cancer as adults.

I was at an angry place in my life, so this new information only fueled my anger. I even said out loud to my husband, "What good does that do me now? It's not like I can go back in time thirty years and join the track club!"

My husband wisely pointed out that this new information could give today's teenage girls added incentive to participate in sports. He also said, "You're absolutely right. You can't go back and do what you should have done thirty years ago, nor can you undo anything you might have done that increased your risk of breast cancer. But you can change what you're doing or not doing today and increase your chances of a better tomorrow."

It took a while, but I worked through the anger, and now I see what I went through as an opportunity to encourage young women to participate in physical activity and maintain a healthy weight throughout their lives in order to reduce their risk of breast cancer and other life-threatening diseases and conditions.

It's important to remember that many risk factors for cancer are unknown and many others are beyond our control, but feeling guilty about the things we've done or not done that may have increased our risk of cancer doesn't do any good; it only wastes valuable time and makes us feel worse than we already do. On the other hand, it is important to know what those things are so that we can change the way we take care of ourselves now.

You can take a little walk today even if you've never been athletic. You can improve the quality of your diet today even if you're overweight. You can stop smoking today even if you've smoked for years. You can wear sunscreen today even if you've been a sun worshipper all your life.

While it's not possible to change the past, isn't it wonderful that we can learn from it and that we can use what we've learned to give ourselves and others a brighter future?

Dear God, I am so grateful for the body you gave me. Sometimes I feel guilty over things I shouldn't have done or should have done to take better care of Your priceless gift. Please help me forgive myself, and show me the way to begin getting stronger today.
~ Amen ~

Most of the important things in the world have been accomplished by people who have kept on trying when there seemed to be no hope at all.

Dale Carnegie

Live Your Dreams, Heal Your Life

reams pass into the reality of action. From the actions stems the dream again; and this interdependence produces the highest form of living.
~ Anais Nin

We've heard many stories of cancer survivors who made drastic changes in their lives with the end result that they lived – and, in many cases, are still living – the rest of their lives doing what they always knew they wanted to do.

A single teacher resigned from her position after being diagnosed with and treated for cancer. She sold all of her belongings and joined the Peace Corps. She's still teaching, but she's teaching women and children in a remote African village to raise crops and livestock so they can become self-sufficient.

A newspaper editor who was told she would probably die within two years of her cancer diagnosis told her husband and their adult children of a fantasy she had held since childhood. With her family's support, she quit her job. She and her husband sold everything and moved to a small village in Italy where she began to study painting with a local master. Today she is a selling artist, living and loving life in the Italian countryside, ten years after she was expected to die. Her husband, formerly a pharmacist, began to indulge his own lifelong fantasy of writing fiction, and has become a successful author.

We know of one gentleman who was hospitalized on a number of occasions and considered near death more than once during his lengthy battle with cancer. He had worked for the railroad for 49 years of his 64 years, but he had harbored a secret fantasy of playing the banjo and becoming an entertainer. On one of his few good days, he decided to indulge his dream as much as possible in what little time was left to him. So his wife found a local banjo player who was willing to come to the house to give him lessons. The last we heard, he was picking and singing his heart out at county fairs and other events up and down the east coast, performing while cloggers dance, and sometimes entertaining audiences solo, singing original songs while accompanying himself on the banjo.

Yes, the people in these examples may still have cancer, but they have far outlived their life expectancies and are living their days joyfully. Many others who have made similar drastic changes in their lifestyles have enjoyed such complete and lengthy remissions of their diseases that they might well be considered cured.

If these kinds of lifestyle changes seem unrealistic or even impossible to you due to your own circumstances, I encourage you to write down your wildest dream and the lifestyle changes that would have to occur in order for you to achieve it. Then break it down into small steps and explore on paper ways in which each step could be taken. Break it down into "baby steps" and you will probably discover that your fantasy isn't so unrealistic after all.

Your fantasies and your dreams are your mind's way of telling you what you really want and what you really should be doing with your life.

Remember that we're talking about healing your life here, *not* curing cancer. There is a huge difference. Treating cancer is for the medical professionals. Healing our lives is for you and me.

We *can* heal our lives even if we have cancer.

Dear God, help me understand that healing my life is not about curing my cancer, and that if I am cured of my cancer, my life will still be in need of healing. Help me remember my dreams, Lord, and to understand that if I am alive today, I can move in the direction of those dreams, even if it means taking just one baby step.
~ Amen ~

Although the world is full of suffering, it is also full of the overcoming of suffering.

Helen Keller

"Oh, hi honey. I was just thinking about you!"

The Great Gorilla Hunt

Fear grows in darkness; if you think there's a bogeyman around, turn on the light.

~ Dorothy Thompson

When I was a very little girl, the neighborhood bully told me that a gorilla had escaped from the zoo and would come into my room that night when I was asleep and eat me alive. I was too young to know there was no zoo within a hundred miles of where we lived or that gorillas don't eat people. The story was terrifying enough and real enough to me that I lay trembling in my bed that night, sobbing into my pillow.

My father heard me crying and came into my room. He sat on the edge of the bed and asked me what was wrong. I told him about the gorilla that had escaped from the zoo and that would surely eat me alive if I fell asleep.

As an adult, I am amazed by the wisdom and restraint my father showed that night. He didn't tell me I was being silly. He didn't say there was no gorilla. He didn't point out there was no zoo within a hundred miles, and he didn't tell me that gorillas don't eat little girls.

Instead, he nodded his head as he listened intently to the fear that spilled out of me. He thought for a few minutes, appearing to consider the situation very seriously, and then announced the only thing to be done was for the two of us to go in search of that gorilla. My father hoisted me onto his shoulders, handed me a flashlight, and together we went out into the night.

We looked everywhere for that gorilla: in the back yard, between the neighboring houses, up and down the street, behind trash cans and under cars. I shone my flashlight up into the trees and in every imaginable dark, scary place. Only when I was completely satisfied there was no gorilla lurking about did my father take me home and tuck me back into my bed. He let me keep the flashlight, just in case.

This cherished childhood memory has often been just the catalyst I needed to make me "turn on the light" when I have been fearful of things that go bump in the night and scary things I could not see or identify. At no time has this been truer or more important than when I have found discolorations on my skin, lumps in strange places and odd or painful sensations here and there on my body. Thanks to my father and "The Great Gorilla Hunt," I know that no matter how frightened I am, the only thing to do is go to the doctor and begin the series of examinations and tests that will answer the question, "What is it?"

As terrifying as it has been to poke around in dark places looking for scary things – and even more so when one hunt uncovered a real "gorilla" – these experiences have taught me some invaluable life lessons: when we turn on the light, we usually find there is nothing there at all; there will always be bullies who try to frighten us (benign lumps and marks); and most gorillas can be captured and tamed.

But we have to find them first.

Heavenly Father, give me the courage to turn on the light when I am afraid of the dark. Help me remember that You are there in the scary places, between the shadows, and in every place I fear to go. Take my hand, Lord, and lead me to where You are.

~ Amen ~

I don't believe I've ever met a person who hasn't been challenged or wounded by something. Difficulties present choices. We can either waste away from our wounds or use them to grow our souls.

Joan Borysenko

God's night school.

God's Night School

*P*eople are like stained-glass windows. They sparkle and shine when the sun is out, but when the darkness sets in their true beauty is revealed only if there is light from within.

~ Elisabeth Kübler-Ross

Without a doubt, the nights were the worst. During the daytime, family and friends visited and chatted. Others called to talk on the phone. My mother rented movies and we watched them together. My teenage sons went through the typical trials and tribulations of that phase of life, and its inherent daily drama kept my thoughts occupied. Visits to the oncology clinic or the radiation therapy center at the hospital provided opportunities to visit with other patients and cheerful nurses and technicians.

And the daylight somehow made everything okay. It was easier to feel upbeat in the daytime, and it was easier to believe I would get well. I didn't feel so alone when the sun was up.

But when night fell, everything changed. The nightmares of childhood were nothing compared to the horrors of those nights. With everyone in our household sound asleep and not a sound to be heard anywhere, I would bolt upright in my bed, my heart pounding. I trembled all over, pulled the blankets tighter around me and lay there shivering and sobbing until the dim light of morning glowed through the curtains.

Then I heard someone refer to such times as "God's Night Classes." He said that God often awakens us in the middle of the night during difficult times for the simple reason that it is quiet then and there is nothing to distract us from communicating with Him. With all around us dark and silent, we can talk to Him and we can listen to what He has to tell us.

I began to look at those nightly wake-up calls as God's Night Classes. When I began to shake all over and the tears came, I begged Him to pull me close, to comfort me and calm my fears. I told Him where it hurt and what I was afraid of.

And, yes, I prayed for a cure. But mostly I just prayed for courage to get through one more treatment, one more surgery, one more day of living with cancer.

After a few of these "classes," the trembling and the tears stopped. If I awoke during the night, I said, "Hello, God. I'm here."

Invariably He said, "So am I."

Dear God, help me to remember that You are always there, not just in the daylight hours, but also in the dark of night. When I feel frightened and alone, pull me close and comfort me. Whisper to me that You are there. Help me to rest, knowing I am safe in Your arms and that you are watching over me through all the days and nights of my life.

~ Amen ~

Along
the Way

A Funny Thing Happened...

L aughter rises out of tragedy, when you need it the most, and rewards you for your courage.   ~ Erma Bombeck

We do a lot of public speaking about our cancer experience, and much of our presentation is, we've been told, "downright hilarious." During the nearly six years we've been doing this, we've spoken at hundreds of cancer related events and to tens of thousands of survivors, caregivers and medical professionals. Every time we've been invited to speak, we were told it was because the meeting planner had heard that we were "very funny" and that our presentation is "uplifting and inspirational." We work hard at being all of those things.

In those six years, exactly two people have commented that they think it is wrong to make jokes when talking about a subject as serious as cancer. And – you guessed it – not only was neither of them a cancer survivor, but neither of them has ever heard us speak publicly or any of our jokes. They had only heard from someone else that we tell jokes when we speak about cancer.

Cancer survivors are the most resilient people we've ever met. The Cancer Crusade receives e-mails, postcards and letters every week from survivors who just want to share something funny that happened to them along their cancer journey. They often end by saying, "By the way, you have my permission to use that." We have used many of their precious, priceless stories in our writing and in our speaking, and we feel truly blessed and honored that they chose to share those treasures with us.

One of the two times someone said something to us about this subject was at a cancer fundraising event (we were not speaking at the event; we were there only as guests). Someone who said he had heard what we do told us it bothered him that we "make fun of cancer." He said he doesn't think cancer is "any laughing matter," and that it is wrong of us and "offensive" to cancer survivors to make jokes about it.

Whoa, Nelly! We reminded him that we are cancer survivors, and we tried to explain that we do not make fun of cancer or those who are fighting it. We told him we agree that cancer is no laughing matter, but that funny things occasionally happen along the cancer journey, and we believe if we can find a way to laugh or smile while fighting cancer, then the hated disease has lost a little of its hold on us and we have been blessed in a mighty way. Humor and laughter are gifts from God, and we were always taught that it's wrong not to use the many gifts He has given us.

But this gentleman would hear none of it. We said a little prayer for him and moved on.

That said, and in defense of the healing powers of humor, I'd like to tell you about a funny thing that happened to me on my way home from the hospital after my third cancer surgery in as many months. And I'll preface the story by saying that if anyone had ever told me it was possible to throw up and laugh at the same time, I wouldn't have believed them. That is, until I experienced it myself.

Roger was helping me up the driveway to our house after driving me home from the hospital. Our two teenaged sons ran out to meet us and to help.

As the three of them fussed over me, I stopped in my tracks, waved a hand in the air and said, "I think I'm going to be sick."

Instantly, I felt three strong pairs of hands on my arms and shoulders, supporting me, holding me, guiding me to the side of the driveway. As sick as I was, the thought crossed my mind that, in spite of everything I was going through on this journey called cancer, I was the luckiest woman alive to have these three caring, compassionate men to love and support me through it all.

As their hands continued to turn me toward the flower bed, my younger son said gently, "Not on the Mustang, Mom."

Take it from me, it *is* possible to throw up and laugh at the same time. It's not pretty, but it's possible.

Yet another reminder that there is beauty even in life's ugliest moments, tenderness in the toughest of times, and humor even in illness. We just have to look for these little blessings, make ourselves open to receiving them, and cherish them when we find them.

Dear God, cancer certainly is no laughing matter. There is nothing funny about what I'm going through or what my family and friends are experiencing as they watch me struggle with my illness. But there are funny things that happen from time to time along this journey, and there are many opportunities to turn uncomfortable situations into occasions for smiles and laughter. Please help me find them and to recognize them when I do, knowing they can make me stronger, knowing they can help me feel better, knowing they are gifts from You to brighten this path I must take.

~ Amen~

If you will call your troubles experiences, and remember that every experience develops some latent force within you, you will grow vigorous and happy, however adverse your circumstances may seem to be.

John R. Miller

Friends

I n prosperity our friends know us; in adversity we know our friends.   ~ John Churton Collins

When I was undergoing chemotherapy, I lost my hair and was often very ill, but one of the most painful side effects to endure was the effect my treatment had on my friends. I watched them struggle to find the right words to say, and I hurt for them. There were times I believed that what I was going through was harder on the people who cared about me than it was on me.

I understood how they felt because I had once been the caregiver for a family member who had been seriously ill for more than a year. Watching someone you love suffer is a truly humbling experience. You want to be there for them, but you don't know what to say and the silences are so awkward. Do you talk about their illness or do you avoid the subject? Do you offer to help them with some physical need and run the risk of hurting them? You just feel all clumsy and tongue-tied when all you want to do is make everything better for them.

Some friends and family members of seriously ill people do the worst thing possible. They stop calling and coming around at all. The conversations and visits become so uncomfortable that they just can't do it anymore.

This is when you as the patient can help make it easier for those who care about you. Tell them what you need and what you want. Is there a CD or tape you'd like to have? Ask someone to get it for you. Maybe a tabletop waterfall would add a tranquil atmosphere to your room. Ask for one. Maybe you're craving hot bread or scrambled eggs or some other dish. Ask for it. Wish someone would give your family a night out? Ask friends to treat your spouse and children to pizza and a movie. Has your room gotten stuffy? Tell a friend you could use some help changing the linens and airing out the room.

Remember that when a friend asks what she can do to help, she really wants to know. Telling her what you need and want sets up a win-win situation for you both: you get what you need or want, and your friend feels like she is really helping you which is all she really wants!

I have a wonderful friend who came to my rescue one night when Roger was out of town and I was alone. I was in pain and needed some medication if I was going to get through the night. I called my friend and told her I needed her. She found an all-night pharmacy, brought me what I needed, and stayed beside me until I felt better. After I recovered, she told me how happy it had made her to be able to do something to help me during my illness.

Dear God, thank you for my friends. They are truly one of Your greatest gifts. My illness is hurting them, too. Please help me find the words to tell them what I need and want.

~ Amen ~

Joy

*W*eeping may endure for a night, but joy cometh in the morning.   ~ Psalms 30:5

After we had completed more than a year of aggressive treatments for our cancers (after being diagnosed within six weeks of one another), we made a list of all the things we wanted to do in whatever time we might have left on this earth, and we began right away to do them. No more of that "maybe someday" stuff for us. Cancer had taught us that "someday" might never come.

We had always wanted to swim with dolphins, so we went to Florida, and we did it. Those incredible creatures were so huge and powerful – so much bigger than I had imagined from photos and film – and yet they were amazingly gentle and playful. They moved through the warm water with us, sprayed and splashed us, "talked" to us and took us on thrilling rides. They clearly enjoyed showing us their beautiful world and teaching us to play in it. It seemed to me they knew we had forgotten how to play, and they used their gentle ways to remind us.

It was an unforgettable day of pure joy. I was breathless with excitement and happier than I had been in years. Roger said my face was "lit like a Christmas tree" all day long.

That day healed me on many levels. Perhaps the most important outcome was that I began to look forward again and to plan what our next joy would be. Instead of indulging in fearful fantasies and dark terrors about what the future might hold, I indulged in rich and exciting daydreams about what I would do the very next day!

After the heady thrill of swimming with the dolphins, I realized that we can make joy happen. We don't have to wait for it. We can identify right now – this very minute – the things that make us joyful, and we can bring them into our lives.

Joy doesn't have to be a destination or an event or even a big deal, but do dream about those and plan for them during treatment and recovery. Make a scrapbook or a collage about your plans; add to it frequently and look at it every day. And as soon as you're up to it, do it!

In the meantime, reflect on – and make lists of – the movies and music that have brought you joy in the past, and en- JOY them again. And again. Re-read a book that delighted you when you were a child. Play a board or card game you haven't played in years. Prepare or request "special occasion" dishes and treats when there is no other special occasion than being alive today.

After all, what could be more joyful than that?

Heavenly Father, I have forgotten what joy feels like.
Too many bad test results, the terrifying waiting, needles
and medicines that hurt and make me sick, scary machines
and hospital stays – these have become the focus of my
days. Help me to refocus, God. Remind me of the simple
joys I once knew, and show me the way to them again.
Lift my head and my heart out of the chemo bed or chair
today, off the radiation or surgery table, and into a place
of rest and peace where I can plan for a joyful future.
~Amen~

The most beautiful people we
have known are those who have
known defeat, known suffering,
known struggle, known loss, and
have found their way out of the depths.
These persons have an appreciation,
a sensitivity and an understanding of
life that fills them with compassion,
gentleness and a deep loving concern.
Beautiful people do not just happen.

Elisabeth Kübler-Ross

Spiritual Healing

W hen you come to the edge of all the light you know and are about to step off into the darkness of the unknown, faith is knowing one of two things will happen: there will be something solid to stand on, or you will be taught how to fly.

~ Patrick Overton

When I was diagnosed with cancer, everything I thought I believed evaporated. Suddenly, nothing was clear anymore. The uncertainty loomed like a huge, dark hole that was sucking me in, and I was no longer sure of anything.

I was angry with everyone around me because I didn't believe they could possibly understand what I was going through. I became especially impatient with those who said, "Hey, you'll probably outlive me! I could be hit by a bus tomorrow!" My answer to that was bitter and sarcastic: "Maybe so, but I can read the license plate of the bus bearing down on me."

If this is where you currently are in your cancer journey, try to be patient with those around you, but above all be patient with yourself. It takes time to come to terms with how your beliefs relate to what you are experiencing now.

Many cancer patients have amazed and inspired me with their overwhelming spiritual faith and their ability to rise above every painful treatment, test and surgery by relying on their religious beliefs. For me, however, it took a lot of soul-searching, reading, counseling and prayer to finally arrive at a place where I am able to embrace my mortality and to understand that it is our very mortality that makes every day and every moment so incredibly precious.

If we were immortal, our days – and ultimately our lives – would become meaningless. Our mortality is a gift, not a punishment!

Remember to devote at least as much time and energy to nurturing and healing your spiritual self as you devote to your physical self. Set aside time each day for prayer and meditation.

Create healing rituals for yourself; these might incorporate the sound of running water or ocean waves, soft music, candles, aromatherapy, or simply a pot of freshly brewed tea.

You may find that a few visits with a pastor, priest, rabbi or other spiritual leader can help bring you to a new level of peace.

Visit your local library or bookstore (in person or online) and browse the sections on religion and spirituality. You will find hundreds of titles from which to choose, and many of them will be in line with the beliefs with which you feel most comfortable.

Dear God, this diagnosis has brought me to the edge of all I ever thought I knew and believed. Please help me to find peace and solace as I travel this path. When I tremble at the thought of yet another surgery or treatment, help me to remember that You are there with me in the treatment room, in the operating room or wherever I am receiving care. I can rest in the knowledge that You are my "something solid to stand on" and, through this cancer experience, You are teaching me to fly.

~ Amen ~

The turning point in the process of growing up is when you discover the core of strength within you that survives all hurt.

Max Lerner

The Healing Power of Music

I think I should have no other mortal wants, if I could always have plenty of music. It seems to infuse strength into my limbs and ideas into my brain. Life seems to go on without effort, when I am filled with music.

~ George Eliot

I spent the summer of the '96 Olympics in chemotherapy. The official theme of the Atlanta games that year was "Reach," an anthem-like song by Grammy winner Gloria Estefan. "Reach" had a driving drumbeat and lyrics that lifted me to a higher place, a place where I felt I could accomplish anything:

"...I'll do whatever it takes,
Follow through with the promise I made,
Put it all on the line,
What I hoped for at last would be mine.
If I could reach, higher,
Just for one moment touch the sky,
From that one moment in my life,
I'm gonna be stronger,
Know that I've tried my very best,
I'd put my spirit to the test...
I'll go the distance this time,
Seeing more the higher I climb,
That the more I believe,
All the more that this dream will be mine..."

I knew the song was for the Olympic athletes, but I made it mine anyway. I listened to it every day, at home, in the car, in the treatment room. I danced to it in my living room ("chair danced" on bad days).

"Put it all on the line," "Put my spirit to the test," and "I'll go the distance this time" were especially meaningful lines for me because they reflected my experience that difficult summer. The music and the lyrics and the percussion were just so...determined. Their powerful combination said to me, "You can do this. You *will* reach higher, and you *will* reach deeper into yourself than you have ever reached, and you *will* find a part of you that you never knew existed, and *that* will be the part of you that will finish this and be victorious. *You will do this*." Every time I heard Gloria belt out "my song," I grew stronger. And since getting stronger was the goal, this was the perfect theme song for me.

Never forget the power of music to affect our moods, and never forget that our bodies respond to our moods. When we're stressed and anxious, soothing music can help calm us, even lull us into restful sleep (as in "lull-aby"). When we're in need of spiritual comfort, music from the religious and cultural traditions we grew up with can provide just the relief we need. And when we're in need of courage, when we're not brave but we want to be, songs about power and determination can open up a part of us we never knew was there.

Since that summer of what I now think of as my own personal Olympic victory, I have collected dozens of other songs (as well as many instrumental pieces and even some opera – now that was a "reach" for me!) that I listen to again and again when I'm in need of courage. Two of my favorites are "I'm Still Standing" by Elton John and "Win" by Brian McKnight.

Begin your own music collection and experience its healing powers. Whether your taste runs to rock 'n roll or gospel, hip hop or classical, choose music with messages of survival, love, courage, faith and beating the odds. Find one special song that makes you feel powerful. Make it your theme song – *your* anthem – and listen to it every day.

Dear God, thank you for the gift of music.
I often forget that it is there, just waiting for me to
open and enjoy. Remind me of this precious gift during
this most difficult time in my life, and lead me to the
music that was written just for me.
~ Amen ~

**Do you know what happens
to scar tissue? It's the strongest
part of the skin.**

Michael R. Mantell

Out of suffering have emerged the strongest souls; the most massive characters are seared with scars.

Edwin H. Chapin

When You Cannot Pray

W hen you cannot pray as you would, pray as
you can.   ~ Dean M. Goulburn

My friend had just been diagnosed with breast cancer. Understandably, her first reaction was shock followed
closely by terror and all that entails: sleeplessness, anxiety,
depression and anger.

What bothered her most, however, was that for the first
time in her life, she was unable to pray.

"I don't know what to say," she confided. "I don't know
what to ask for. I can't find the words."

I assured her she was not alone. I had also found it difficult to pray when I was first diagnosed with cancer. My
biggest problem was anger. I was mad at God. He had allowed this awful thing to happen to me, and I didn't want to
talk to Him anymore!

But as the shock and terror slowly wore off and I en-
tered into my year-long cancer journey filled with multiple
surgeries, chemotherapy and radiation treatments, my anger
ebbed, too.

I realized that God had not given me cancer. A mis-
fire at the cellular level had given me cancer. A bad gene,
maybe. Pesticide exposure, perhaps. Whatever had caused
it, it wasn't God. It was biology run amok.

God was right where He had always been, waiting patiently for me to come to Him and lay my burdens at His feet. He knew my fears better than anyone, and He wanted to strengthen and encourage me. All I had to do was come into His presence and ask.

He also knew that I couldn't find the words to ask for what I needed. I wasn't even sure what I needed, so how could I pray?

It was then that He reminded my of the simple bedtime prayer I had prayed as a child. "Now I lay me down to sleep. I pray Thee, Lord, my soul to keep. If I should die before I wake, I pray Thee, Lord, my soul to take."

He also reminded me of the Lord's prayer: "Our Father, who art in heaven, hallowed be thy name."

I realized that my prayers didn't need to be original to be heard. In fact, God has given us many prayers that we need only to read or recall according to our own faith traditions.

Sometimes I just said, "God, I am so scared and so tired that I don't even know how to pray anymore." Then I would sit quietly and wait. Invariably, God spoke to me through my heart. He reminded me that prayer is a two-way street and that sometimes all we have to do is be quiet and listen. Let Him do the talking! Listening is prayer, too.

God is there even in – maybe *especially* in – the silence when we are still and quiet.

God, help me to remember that prayer is a
conversation with You and that sometimes all I
need to do is listen. Remind me that, even when
I'm silenced by terror and can find no words at all,
You can hear what is in my heart.
~ Amen ~

128

*The real glory is being knocked to
your knees and then coming back.
That's real glory. That's the
essence of it.*

Vince Lombardi

"You really need to stop doing that."

How I Learned to Laugh Again

And we should consider every day lost on which we have not danced at least once. And we should call every truth false which was not accompanied by at least one laugh.

~ Friedrich Nietzsche

The steamy August afternoon was just about more than I could take. Sitting in my car at a red light, I was nauseated from my recent chemotherapy treatment, in pain from other cancer medications, and depressed from the whole cancer experience. All I wanted was to finish my errands, go home and crawl into bed.

Noticing that my wig felt lopsided, I took advantage of the red light to look into the rear view mirror. I tugged on the sides and front of the wig to straighten it and saw – to my horror and embarrassment – four teenagers in the car behind me mocking my movements! They were modeling in exaggerated fashion the primping of a vain woman posing before a mirror, and they were laughing themselves silly.

Tears of anguish welled up in my eyes. *How could they be so cruel?* I wondered. *How could they make fun of a sick woman, a woman who might even be dying?*

131

Because they don't know, I quickly answered myself. *And besides, they're just kids. They don't know any better.*

Then I thought... *but they should.*

I don't know where it came from – maybe I was delirious from the heat – but a giggle bubbled up inside me and, without another thought, I placed my hand on top of my head and yanked off my wig. Still looking in the mirror, I gave a huge shrug of my shoulders and laughed out loud just as the light turned green.

The look of total shock on those four teenagers' faces as I pulled away from the intersection will stay with me forever. All four had their hands to their cheeks, and their mouths and eyes were as big and round as dinner plates. I can still hear the horns of other cars blaring at them to move as they sat there stunned and motionless.

I laughed for three days, and for the most part, I haven't stopped laughing since because what I discovered that day was that the physical act of laughing didn't just lighten my mood – it made me feel *physically* better.

Laughter improves your cardiovascular system in much the same way as aerobic exercise. It oxygenates your entire body. Laughter releases endorphins (the "feel good" chemicals) in your brain. Physical discomforts are minimized almost immediately and – even better – your immune system is strengthened. Not only is your body better able to withstand the rigors of any medical treatment you might be undergoing, but it is also better able to fight disease on its own in the ways God and nature intended. Every time you laugh, you become physically healthier, and you ensure that you will be even healthier tomorrow.

Dear God, help me find opportunities to smile and laugh today. Remind me and those around me that humor is a gift from You, a gift designed to lift our hearts and spirits above the pain we all must endure in this lifetime. Bless those who are unable to laugh for they are suffering far more than we can know. Open their hearts, Lord, as you are opening mine, and when they are ready, allow me to share a smile with them.

~ Amen ~

**We must learn from life
how to suffer it.**

French proverb

Our greatest glory consists not in never falling, but in rising every time we fall.

Ralph Waldo Emerson

Pay It Forward

We can do no great things, only small things with great love. ~ Mother Teresa

I had just completed six months of chemotherapy for breast cancer and was facing twenty-five radiation treatments. The radiation oncologist explained that a technician would be making some marks on my body in preparation for the treatments.

When I met with the technician, I tried to cover my nervousness with jokes. She explained that she would be giving me two small tattoos that would look like dots from a ballpoint pen. I laughed and said it was a shame they couldn't be something pretty like roses or hearts. She just smiled and went to work.

When she finished, she helped me sit up and gave me a hand mirror. There on my chest was a beautiful pink rose "tattoo"! It was the rub-on type, of course, but the significance of the gesture took my breath away.

This technician in this cold, tile-and-steel treatment center had done something supremely human and gentle for me during a time when I needed it most. I will never forget her or her generous spirit. Her sweet and simple act of kindness was a shining example of the many life lessons my cancer experience would teach me in the months and years to come.

From that experience I learned that kindness doesn't have to be difficult or expensive or time-consuming. Kindness only means looking at a fellow human being and asking yourself what meaningful gesture you can make to help him along in his journey.

Dear God, it's sometimes hard for me to notice and appreciate the kindness of others during this scary time in my life. I pray that You will calm my spirit so I may be more aware and grateful. And, when I am able, help me discover ways in which to extend kindness to others who are in need. Please help me to remember always that You work through us and that we touch others with Your love and grace every time we reach out to one another in kindness.

~ Amen ~

Adversity often activates a strength we did not know we had.

Joan Walsh Anglund

Some minds seem almost to create themselves, springing up under every disadvantage and working their solitary but irresistible way through a thousand obstacles.

Washington Irving

The Best Dollar
I Ever Spent

*A*ll life is an experiment... The more experiments *you* make the better. What if you...get fairly rolled in the dirt once or twice? Up again, you shall never be so afraid of a tumble.

~ Ralph Waldo Emerson

Shortly before starting my chemotheraphy treatments, my doctor offered me the opportunity to participate in a clinical trial. He didn't use the term "guinea pig", but that's how I saw it. It didn't matter, though. I wanted every available weapon to fight my battle, and the knowledge that I might be able to help further research into treatment options in some small way might give me a sense of purpose, I thought. So I eagerly accepted.

The actual treatments using the trial drug began months later. The drug was brutal, but by that time, I was beginning to understand the healing power of humor. Some previous incidents that had sparked spontaneous laughter had surprised me by making me feel *physically* better, so I had begun actively searching for ways to make myself and others laugh.

I went to one of those everything-costs-a-dollar stores browsing for something to amuse myself. I found a small face mask that was just a rubber nose with whiskers. It looked like a mouse's nose. Or maybe a rat's. *Or maybe a guinea pig's.*

At my next appointment with my oncologist, I sat on the table in the examining room wearing the standard lovely gown, my new nose and whiskers, and a terribly serious expression (keep in mind I was completely bald by then – what a picture, huh?). When my doctor walked in – his head down as he studied my chart – he asked, "And how are you doing today?"

I said, "I don't know about this clinical trial, Doc. I'm starting to feel like a guinea pig."

With a concerned and puzzled expression, he looked up at me. A smile spread slowly across his face. Then he chuckled. Then he started laughing. He laughed so hard he had to sit down. I laughed so much my sides hurt and tears rolled down my face. That rubber nose was the best dollar I ever spent.

Whether you spend a dime or a dollar or nothing at all, find a way to laugh every day. It truly is an investment in your health.

Dear God, I have lost my sense of humor somewhere amidst the devastation of this disease. Please help me find it again and to remember that laughter is one of Your greatest gifts to us. Show me how to use humor to heal my spirit and to comfort those around me.

~ Amen ~

If you stop struggling,
then you stop life.

Huey Newton

What's So Funny?

*The human race has one really effective weapon,
and that is laughter.* ~ Mark Twain

About mid-way through eight months of aggressive cancer treatments, I found myself – emotionally and spiritually – in the darkest place I'd ever been.

My once long and beautiful strawberry blonde hair was gone. It had always been the one thing about me that stood out, the only feature anyone had ever called "pretty."

Losing my hair was bad enough, but what had really brought me low was the *combination* of all the little surprises cancer treatment offers. No need to go into them all here. If you're reading this, you know what I'm talking about! Suffice to say I no longer looked like myself, and I no longer felt like myself. I didn't know who I was anymore, and I had no idea what the future held or even if I *had* a future.

So cut to me, bald, swollen, and hooked up to IV infusions of drugs that will keep me bald and swollen for months to come. I feel like crap, and I'm making darned sure everyone around me feels like crap, too. I had become a truly evil and frightening woman.

Suddenly, my husband enters the room, grinning like a Cheshire cat, holding something behind his back.

"What's so funny?" I snarled at him.

"Honey, you know I've always told you you should have been a cover girl?" he asked sweetly.

"You're a really sick and twisted man," I said. "Now, of all times, to say something like that."

"No, really!" he said as he came close to the bed. "I've always meant that. I've always thought you were more beautiful than any cover girl. Now I know I was right! You made it! You really *are* a cover girl!"

And he pulled from behind his back a supermarket tabloid with a big headline about the "discovery" of a "giant alien baby" and, sure enough, there was a picture of a baby on the cover that looked – yes, I have to admit it – remarkably like me: bald, swollen immensely (thanks, I'm sure, to a wide angle lens and other photo technology) and, as it was screaming its rather large head off, apparently quite angry.

It's a good thing those IV needles and tubes were securely attached because I laughed so hard I nearly rolled off the bed. I was absolutely convulsed with laughter. I laughed so hard I was crying. And every time I nearly got myself under control, I looked at the tabloid cover and began again. The harder and longer I laughed, the more my husband laughed, too. We rolled on the bed together, laughing hysterically, for at least a half hour.

When we finally pulled ourselves together, I couldn't believe how much better I felt! My anger, anxiety and depression were gone, my breathing was deeper, my pain and nausea were lessened. I was energized, too, and felt like getting out of bed and moving around. It was like I had taken a magic pill!

Like all good magic pills, my laugh attack brought only temporary relief, but the important thing was that the relief it brought was *real* and I could find that relief again and again and again, anytime I needed it, by learning to lighten up.

Sure, there are times and circumstances when there is nothing even remotely funny, but those times are rare. We can usually find something to smile about if we look hard enough.

Dear God, please help me to remember that
You have given us the precious gift of laughter. Help
me find humor in the little everyday aggravations of life
as well as the truly difficult times. Remind me to smile,
remind me to laugh, and help me always to help
others do the same.
~ Amen ~

I bend, but I do not break.

Jean de La Fontaine

*People's best successes come
after their disappointments.*

Henry Ward Beecher

What's So Funny – Part Deux

*L*aughter *is higher than all pain.*
~ Elbert Hubbard

Laughter *is* good medicine. This is not voodoo, folks. This is the real deal. There is scientific evidence that suggests it lowers blood pressure, gives you a great cardio workout and can even boost your immune system. In one study, laughter was found to increase the pain tolerance of children undergoing treatment for cancer! I mean, how great is that? The studies are ongoing, but suffice to say there is enough evidence that you and I need to make laughter a part of our lives every day if we possibly can.

Here are some ideas that can help you laugh, even when you don't feel like it.

- Keep a "Ha Ha" notebook. When you see or hear something that makes you smile or laugh, write it down, draw a picture of it, or cut it out and paste it in.

- Get a mini-recorder and record jokes (if you're like me, you can never remember them). Get children to record their favorite jokes and silly songs for you to play back later, or "interview" them with questions like, "What would you do if you were President of the United States?" Ask them what it means to be in love. You'll get some poignant answers and you'll get some that will make you roll off the bed laughing!

- Keep a camera handy and take pictures of things that strike you as funny.
- Watch, read and listen to funny tapes, books and CDs.
- Watch television sit-coms and those "funniest videos" specials.
- Give a kitten or puppy a piece of ribbon or blow bubbles for them.
- Play peek-a-boo with a toddler.

There is even a school of thought that advocates making yourself laugh even when – no, especially when – you don't feel like it. Don't wait for something funny, these folks say. Pretend you are an actor on stage and the script calls for you to laugh long and hard. Then do it. This is the fake- it-'til-you-can-make-it line of thinking, and it really does work. After a few tries, you will find that your mood responds to your body's laughter.

Likewise, avoid sad, scary and violent television shows, movies and books. Not only are you what you eat; you are also what you read and observe. You're taking better care of yourself now, remember? Take into your body, mind and spirit only those things that nurture and heal!

Dear God, teach me to laugh again. Remind me that, even in these difficult days, when so much is uncertain and frightening, there is exquisite beauty all around me. Remind me that I can find laughter and joy in that beauty if I slow down and observe. You have given me so much to enjoy. Sometimes I just need to be reminded to open up my spirit and see it. Lift me up, Lord, and show me what You see so that I may smile once more.

~ Amen ~

Mother Knows Best

*H*ave courage for the great sorrows of life and patience for the small ones; and when you have laboriously accomplished your daily task, go to sleep in peace. God is awake. ~ Victor Hugo

Most of us have questioned the existence of God at some time in our lives. We have asked where God was on 9/11, during Hurricane Katrina and the tsunami unleashed by the earthquake in the Indian Ocean and other huge catastrophes that have dealt deathblows to entire populations. And we have asked where God was when a personal tragedy occurred, when we have received a diagnosis of a life-threatening disease or condition, or when a loved one lay dying.

I've asked these questions myself during the worst times of my life (including the death of my 34-year old brother; my husband's cancer diagnosis and – six weeks later – my own cancer diagnosis; and several illnesses and conditions that have threatened the lives of my sons), and I have often found comfort in the memory of a simple exchange that took place between my mother and me many years ago.

I was 5 or 6 years old, and I asked my mother where God was. She answered, "Everywhere." I remember being astonished by her answer! *Everywhere?* Yes, she assured me – *everywhere*. I recall asking lots of questions after that, mostly silly ones like *Is He in my ear?* and *Is He in the bathroom?* And my mother answered simply, "Yes." And I believed her.

There are times in our lives when it is easy to believe: a baby is born, a loved one's or our own health is restored, spring returns. And there are times when it is far from easy, when it seems there could be no worse news than what we have just received or when we bear witness to planes that crash into buildings or walls of water that sweep people out to sea.

But it seems to me that if we believe He is in the delivery room when that baby is born and the sickroom when someone who is ill recovers and in the rosebush when the first buds appear in spring, then we must also acknowledge that He is there in the examining room when we get a terrifying diagnosis and at the bedside of a loved one as he slips away and in the planes and the towers and the water. He is in the darkest, scariest places we can imagine. He is in the silence when there are no words big enough to describe our pain.

To deny His existence at these times is to deny every joyful moment we have ever known and to toss those moments off as random products of chaos. God does not play Hide-and-Seek. He is indeed everywhere, and He grieves with us when nature wreaks havoc on our lives and cells run amok in our bodies and men turn His gift of free will into weapons of mass destruction.

If you don't believe me, just ask my mother.

Dear God, I am in despair. My life is filled with shadows and dark corners, and I am afraid. Though there are many around me, I feel alone. I know in my mind that You are there and that You care about what is happening to me, but in my fear and desperation, it is my heart that stuggles to believe. Take me as a child, Lord, and help me find again the simple faith I had when I was small. Remind me that it is in times like this that I must bring my doubts and fears to You as a child shows her mother where it hurts and asks for her healing touch. Remind me yet again that I am Your child and that I have nothing to fear because I am in Your eternal care.

~ Amen ~

Fall seven times, stand up eight.

Japanese proverb

*People are never helped in their
suffering by what they think for
themselves, but only by revelation
of a wisdom greater than their own.
It is this which lifts them out
of their distress.*

C.G. Jung

Reflections on
the Journey

Every Day Is Thanksgiving Day

by Roger Cawthon

*I*f the only prayer you ever say in your whole life is "thank you," that would suffice. ~ Meister Eckhart

Many have called former New York City Mayor Rudy Guliani "America's Mayor" for his courageous leadership on 9/11 and throughout the horrifying days that followed. I'll never forget the photographs of the mayor striding confidently through the rubble that had been the World Trade Center towers, comforting the injured and terrified, thanking the firefighters, police officers and aid workers. When he put his arms around those who had lost loved ones on that most awful of days, his compassionate touch reached out to every American and reminded us that we were all in this together and that there were people in charge who would work hard to make things right again.

I recently had the opportunity to hear Mr. Guliani speak. I expected he would talk about 9/11, terrorism and how we must find new and better ways to fight the epidemic of hatred and violence that threaten our world.

I think he did mention those things. No, I'm sure he did, but I don't remember much of what he said about them. I don't remember much about those words because there were others that meant so much more to me personally, words that hit me like the proverbial ton of bricks that day and will resonate within me for the rest of my life.

He said that his battle with prostate cancer had been a blessing because hearing the diagnosis gave him the opportunity to go home and hug his loved ones, to tell them how much he loved them and how thankful he was to have them in his life.

The victims of 9/11, he pointed out, never had that chance. Three thousand people got up on a beautiful, clear September morning and left their homes to go to work or board airplanes or run errands, ordinary outings for most on what was to be a most extraordinary day, ordinary outings from which they would never return. How many of them, we wonder, had unfinished personal business? How many walked out the door without speaking to the husband or wife they had argued with the night before? How many left a crying child reaching out for one more hug? How many hadn't spoken to a family member for weeks, months, years because of some disagreement that had been allowed to smolder?

He was thankful for his diagnosis of cancer, said Guliani, because it gave him a chance to be more thankful every single day! It reminded him to savor the many blessings in his life and to love his loved ones harder and more deeply than ever before.

Yesterday was Thanksgiving, and being thankful is on most everyone's minds right now. I have always loved Thanksgiving Day for many reasons. I love the food and the football. I love family and friends. I love getting up early and watching the Macy's Thanksgiving Day Parade. I was in the Macy's Thanksgiving Day Parade once when I was a young man, and it holds a special place in my memories and in my heart. I still get excited when Santa Claus comes into view. I love gathering around the table covered with wonderful food, and I love the ritual of saying the special grace. I love having the day off and lying around the house, stomach too full, and napping. I love napping and I hardly ever get to do it, except on Thanksgiving Day.

We have a tradition on Thanksgiving Day that I especially love. In the evening, my wife, Kathy, and I pick up my sister, Mary, and her two beautiful daughters, Tina and Amy, and we take a drive through the local park's "Celebration In Lights." We always go through twice. We turn on the radio and sing along (our motto is "If you can't be good, be loud!") to the holiday songs. This year we took some hot chocolate along for the ride. I loved that.

I love my wife on Thanksgiving Day. Don't get me wrong, I love my wife every day. But I especially love her on Thanksgiving Day because she makes Thanksgiving Day, and every holiday, so very special. My wife loves holidays and she gives them a special "feel" with her enthusiasm. She always decorates and plays music and bounces around the house being happy. And she makes everyone else happy. I love that.

I love Thanksgiving Day for a lot of reasons. But, mostly I love Thanksgiving Day because it reminds me to be thankful. Not just thankful for the food, although I always am. And not just thankful for family and friends who are so near and dear to me. No, it reminds me to be thankful for life itself.

You see, Thanksgiving Day has a way of making me stop, for just a moment, and reflect, really reflect on the many blessings that I have in my life. They say you should count your blessings, but I have too many to count, too many to name them all. My wife, Kathy, our sons, my mom and dad and brothers and sister, many nieces and nephews, and MeMa and DeDa, and football, and music, and turkey, and that breath of air that I just took, and life itself. And my God.

It wasn't always that way. There was a time when I wasn't quite so thankful. Like Rudy Guliani and millions of other Americans, I will never forget hearing the words, "You have cancer." My life, as I knew it, ceased to exist, and was immediately replaced with one filled with confusion, questions and doubt. Doubt about everything, including my God.

But my doubt did not last very long. After the initial shock, the awful diagnosis began to work a strange kind of transformational magic. It reminded me on a daily basis – now and forever – that I have so much to be thankful for. I am alive, at least for now. I am still standing, my wife at my side. I am thankful for that.

And I still have my God. Always did, of course. What is it they say? "If you don't feel close to God, guess who moved." I am very thankful for that.

I am thankful for the chance I was given. I had a chance to survive, even if just for another day. And that was enough to be thankful for.

My wife says that there are two kinds of people in the world, those who "get it" and those who don't. Suddenly, I "got it." Everything had changed and it was okay.

It shouldn't be this way, but it seems it takes some kind of life-altering event to make people get it. The people who miraculously walked out of the Twin Towers in New York City told TV reporters that they were going to go home and hug their wives and kids. Suddenly, they got it. A diagnosis of cancer, or any life-threatening illness, suddenly makes you so aware of life, and time, and, everything. And you appreciate it. You finally appreciate everything. And you are so thankful for whatever time you have been granted. You become so thankful. You get it.

For me, every day is Thanksgiving Day.

Dear God, Thank you.
~ Amen ~

Good people are good because they've come to wisdom through failure.

William Saroyan

"I've decided to live every day like it's my last,
and I'm NOT cleaning house on my last day!"

After the Storm

I am not afraid of storms, for I am learning how to sail my ship. ~ Louisa May Alcott

Three years ago, our area was devastated by a powerful hurricane. While – thankfully – it didn't have the tragic consequences of Hurricane Katrina, our entire region was without power for days on end, and most residents had no electricity for several weeks. Hot water and ice became luxuries overnight.

The clean-up effort was massive. Huge trees were downed along major highways and city roads; chainsaws roared for days as fallen and uprooted vegetation was hacked to pieces.

Debris from the storm was everywhere, and the mountains of wreckage grew ever larger as residents began to empty homes that had been flooded. Homeowners dragged ruined furnishings out to the street, pulled up soaked carpets and hauled them to the curb, carried boxes of once-treasured belongings – keepsakes now destroyed by wind and water – and placed them on the street for city workers to bury in a landfill.

When people took breaks from the monumental tasks at hand, they wandered around their neighborhoods in shock and disbelief at the extent of the destruction. Neighbors shared their stories with one another and – as often happens after a community suffers a collective blow – those who had food, drinking water, hot showers and ice began to share those things with those who did not.

And so, slowly but surely, we began to recover from the hurricane's wrath.

As we worked through the end of summer and into the early fall, we began to notice the most amazing recovery of all. Flowering bushes and trees that should have been finished blooming for the year suddenly flourished, becoming heavy with full, fragrant, brilliantly colored blossoms. Six weeks later, the trees that had withstood the storm's howling winds burst into dazzling fall colors, more spectacular than any we could remember. Every bush and shrub, every tree from sapling to ancient oak seemed to shout, "I'm here! I made it through! And look how much better I am for having survived the storm!"

Mother Nature had given us a lesson in pruning. By stripping herself of excess, she had made those parts that remained stronger, hardier and infinitely more beautiful than they had been before.

Cancer is like a hurricane that blows through our lives, forcing us to take stock of what is important and real. It makes us clear out the dead wood and tangled branches of our lives and strips us down to the very core of who and what we truly are. It compels us to discard the irrelevant, fix the broken and shore up the weak places in our hearts, minds and spirits.

We can take comfort in knowing that, when the storm has passed, what we are will be better than what we were.

Dear God, help me to see my disease as a storm blowing though my life, each treatment as just a brief squall, painful symptoms and side effects as sudden, drenching downpours that will soon be over. Help me to visualize, believe and understand that, though my body may be ravaged and broken, my spirit will be stronger, hardier and infinitely more beautiful after the pruning.

~ Amen ~

I will face my fear. I will permit it to pass over me and through me. And when it has gone past, I will turn the inner eye to see its path. Where the fear has gone there will be nothing. Only I will remain.

Frank Herbert

Life is not about waiting for the storm to pass. It's about learning to dance in the rain.

Unknown

Overcoming Survivor Guilt

*W*hy should a dog, a horse, a rat, have life,
And thou no breath at all?
~ William Shakespeare, <u>King Lear</u>

While I was fighting for my own life, I lost one of my best friends to cancer. Her name was "Juanita." The Spanish name is the feminine form of "Juan" which means "God is gracious." After her death at age 34, I doubted very much and for quite a long time that God is gracious, since my dictionary defines that word as "displaying divine grace, mercy, or compassion."

There had been other losses in my life. The worst was that of my own brilliant, sweet and handsome brother – my only sibling – who also died at the age of 34. There was the young woman with whom I taught who went to bed one night, seemingly the picture of health, and never awakened. And there was the infant son of a neighbor who picked up a nasty infection that took his tiny life in a matter of a few days.

But it was Juanita's death that caused me to experience "survivor's guilt" for the first time, probably because we had similar diagnoses. Why had cancer taken her and not me? I almost laughed when I heard people say that "life isn't fair" because "fair" is such a wimp of a word to use when taking in the immense mysteries of life and death and when considering our poor attempts to find some shred of meaning in all of it. After all, as Johnny Carson once said, "If life were fair, Elvis would be alive and all the impersonators would be dead."

In the years following Juanita's death, there was much talk about survivor's guilt and much material available on the subject because of events in the news. Most of us felt a bit of its sting when a riding accident left Christopher Reeve's "Superman" body broken and paralyzed; when a car carrying Princess Diana smashed into the wall of a tunnel in Paris; when an ill-fated flight took the life of John F. Kennedy, Jr. and his wife and sister-in-law; when the unthinkable, the unspeakable happened on 9/11 and the walls of our last illusions came tumbling down, finally and forever.

But for all the material I have come across in the years since Juanita's death, all the books published on the subject of survivor's guilt, all the television talk show interviews with experts, I find that I return time and again to the most profoundly comforting book I have ever read. *When Bad Things Happen to Good People*, by Harold S. Kushner, is a small volume, just over 150 pages, easily read in a few hours. I encourage you to purchase a copy, read it and keep it close so that you can read it again and again, anytime you find yourself going to that life-isn't-fair place and wondering why you are still here when someone you loved and cherished is not.

I also encourage you to celebrate the ones you have lost and to keep the flames of their lives shining brightly by giving something good and beautiful to the world with your own life. It doesn't have to be big, but it has to come from a big place in your heart. It doesn't have to be expensive, but it must be generous of spirit.

I won't even begin to list the possibilities because they would be my ideas and not yours, and because once I started to list them, I would never be able to stop. *You* start. *You* think. *You* dream. *You* imagine. *You* leave a legacy.

Do it in memory of the loved ones you have lost. And do it so that, when you are gone, the world will be twice blessed by your having been a part of it.

For everything there is a season,
    and a time for every matter under heaven:
A time to be born, and a time to die;
A time to plant,
    and a time to pluck up what is planted;
A time to kill, and a time to heal;
A time to break down, and a time to build up;
A time to weep, and a time to laugh;
A time to mourn, and a time to dance;
A time to throw away stones,
    and a time to gather stones together;
A time to embrace,
    and a time to refrain from embracing;
A time to seek, and a time to lose;
A time to keep, and a time to throw away;
A time to tear, and a time to sew;
A time to keep silence, and a time to speak;
A time to love, and a time to hate,
A time for war, and a time for peace.
            Ecclesiastes 3:1-8

Fear is that little darkroom
where negatives are developed.

Michael Pritchard

Another Type of Survivor Guilt

*I*n the depth of winter, I finally learned that there was within me an invincible summer.

~ Albert Camus

A subscriber wrote to us: "My sister and I have cancer. Our six siblings are healthy. We both feel guilty for having cancer...like we are putting the family through so much...Is it a feeling of being punished for something bad? We don't think so, and yet we can't help but feel bad when we talk to our healthy siblings about our (diagnoses). If you have felt the same way, or if you understand what I mean, I'd appreciate it if you'd share with me."

We decided this was a great topic for an affirmation because it describes feelings that all of us survivors have experienced at one time or another, those feelings of being a burden to our families and friends, of dragging them down somehow, feelings that if it weren't for us and all of our health problems, they would have happy lives.

I'd like to address these feelings by sharing two experiences that have helped me deal with my own feelings of this particular type of survivor's guilt.

When I was in chemotherapy 11 years ago, I spent quite a few months in my house because I was just too sick to go out. Most of the time I was in bed or on the couch just being very still and quiet. Bless her heart, my mother spent most of those long miserable days with me. She rented movies and watched them with me. She cleaned our house, did the laundry, fixed meals, rode herd on the kids, and did whatever else she could to keep our lives running smoothly while I rested and healed. She may not know this to this day, but I watched her as she cared for me. I watched her face and I watched her eyes, and I saw the fear she tried so hard to hide from me.

You see, we had already lost my brother, my only sibling, just a few years before. I knew my mother was terrified of losing me, too, her other one, her only surviving child. And I was overcome with guilt during those days. Oh, God, how I did not want to be putting my mother through that!

Today the situation is reversed. Both of my parents have been diagnosed with cancer. Thank goodness the prognosis is excellent for both of them, but each must undergo surgeries and treatments that are frightening and uncomfortable. I will be there for them. I will do whatever I can to make this journey less frightening and more tolerable for them. While this is not an opportunity I would have chosen, I am grateful that I can be there for my parents in their time of need.

To everything, there *truly* is a season, and a time for every purpose under heaven.

The other experience occurred on a recent weekend getaway. Roger and I were watching a spectacular sunset over the Albermarle Sound on the Outer Banks of North Carolina. It was the end of what had been a truly glorious day, weather-wise. Suddenly, in spite of the awesome beauty I was witnessing, I was overcome with deep sadness. A friend of ours, a young, vibrant wife and mother, had died very suddenly and unexpectedly just the week before.

Another friend, a competitive athlete in excellent condition, had just been diagnosed with cancer. And the horrific event at Virginia Tech (where many of our friends have children and grandchildren) in which 32 students and staff members lost their lives had happened only a few weeks before.

I said to Roger, "I feel guilty sitting here enjoying this beautiful evening when so many people we know and love are in so much pain."

He said, "Don't *ever* feel guilty about being alive and happy! Everyone's life is filled with sorrow and joy, but thank God we all experience them at different times. When we were battling our cancers, others were having babies, winning lotteries, getting promotions, taking cruises and experiencing happy times. For most people on most days, happy times are much simpler, like enjoying a beautiful sunset. And tonight it's our turn."

He was right, of course, and his words served to remind me of another aspect of this whole "survivor's guilt" issue. I've always cringed when someone says to me, "God won't give you more than you can handle." I refuse to believe that God gave me cancer, and I refuse to believe he gave cancer to my marathon-running friend or my best girlfriend or my mother or my father or my aunts or anyone else. God didn't take our other beautiful young friend suddenly and without warning from her husband and children and countless others who loved her. And God didn't direct the mentally ill young man in Blacksburg to shoot and kill his fellow students and their teachers and then himself.

Bad things happen to good people. It has nothing to do with punishment or anything other than the fact that our biologies sometimes go haywire and we get sick, in our bodies and in our minds; horrible accidents happen in spite of all conceivable precautions; and evil really does exist in the world, in the hearts and minds of others who walk among us.

No, God does not give us what we can handle.

God helps us handle what we are given.

When we are healthy and joyful, we can give to others who are hurting. And when our time of sorrow and sickness comes again – as it will and must, for that is the nature of life – those who are healthy and joyful can care for us. And we can accept it *without guilt*, for our turn will come to give again. And so it goes...

Dear God, please lift this burden of guilt from me. Help me to remember that those who are caring for me during my time of need are doing so because they love me and want to help. Remind me that You are working through them. Make me grateful and gracious in accepting their assistance, their words of comfort, their acts of love. For it is in loving and caring for one another that we embody Your love for us on this earth.

~ Amen ~

Whoever survives a test, whatever
it may be, must tell the story.
That is his duty.

Elie Wiesel

Be the Daffodil

*D*affy-down-dilly came up in the cold... although the white snow lay in many a place.

~ Anna B. Warner

Well, everybody is talking about the weather, and even more so than usual. Parts of the country that have seldom seen even a flake of snow are dealing with many inches of the white stuff. Other parts of the country that are usually covered with ice and snow this time of year are seeing buds on trees and daffodils shooting up through the ground.

Weather experts disagree as to whether this is yet another sign of global warming or whether it's just an *el nino* year. It certainly gives all of us much to think about in terms of the big picture and our precious environment.

In the meantime it has made me think about daffodils.

I love daffodils, and I'm not even what you would call a "flower person." For me, they are just the happiest little guys, and when the ones in the bed in front of our house bloom each year, I run out to greet them with camera in hand.

No matter how much snow has covered them, no matter how many bitterly cold nights have settled upon them, no matter how many ice storms have beaten and battered the ground above them, invariably and without fail, they shove their bright little faces up out of the earth and turn toward the sun as if to say, "Ha! Here I am! You didn't think I could do it this time, but in spite of it all, I'm still here!"

No wonder the daffodil is the traditional flower symbol for cancer survivors. We endure the shock of diagnosis, the dread of surgeries and other treatments, the painful and often disabling side effects, and the fearful uncertainty that follows us the rest of our lives, because now we *truly* understand. We really and finally get it –

> that life is about
> hills and valleys,
> triumph and defeat,
> storms and sunshine
> and yet...
> and yet...
> and yet...
> we keep on keepin' on.

We are the daffodils.

*Dear God, be with me as I weather the storms of this disease. Lift me up above the surgical table and the treatment bed or chair, beyond the confines of the hospital and the clinic and my sick bed at home. Raise me higher than the storms and all the places they rage, both within and without. And even **as** they rage, Lord, remind me to give thanks for storms because it takes both sunshine and showers to make little yellow flowers grow.*

~ Amen ~

Dark Valleys And Hilltop Hours

The hilltop hour would not be half so wonderful if there were no dark valleys to traverse.

~ Helen Keller

The day of my last radiation treatment was one of the most joyful days of my life. It was graduation from one of the toughest schools there is: Cancer U.

I had looked forward to this day for nearly a year, and I had planned it. I wanted to go to the hospital alone; this was a joy that no one I knew could understand, so I wanted to celebrate it by myself. Anyone else might think I was nuts.

When I got into my car to leave the hospital for the last time, I put a cassette tape in the tape player. The trumpets announced the "Theme From Rocky" and, with the music blaring, I drove home happier than I could ever remember having been, short of the two times I had given birth and the day my husband and I were married.

Since that day I have had other joyful moments: watching a friend's daughter fall in love and plan a wedding; seeing our sons succeed in school and business; hearing our niece announce her pregnancy; crossing the finish line of a marathon.

Some of the most joyful moments were quiet ones that caught me off guard and took my breath away with their simple yet profound beauty. That moment when the family is finally seated around a holiday table, when I look around at those I love and am moved almost to tears as I give thanks that we are together once again. The magical second or two when a butterfly lights on my shoulder. The first leaf that flutters to the ground in the fall. The last instants of wakefulness at night when my husband squeezes my hand and whispers, "I love you."

Of course I had the same or similar experiences before I was diagnosed with cancer, but now my highs are higher. Whenever a joyful moment is upon me, I stop whatever else I am doing and just bask in it like a cat in a sunny window. I allow my joy to find whatever outlet it will, including hugs, laughter and tears. I no longer worry that people will think I'm strange or silly. In fact, I feel sorry for people who can't or won't express joyfulness.

Another difference in before and after cancer is that my lows are not as low. Everything is in perspective now. I am able to see everything in the context of the big picture. I understand now that the end of the caterpillar's life is just the beginning of a new and better one waiting on the other side of a beautiful and mysterious process of transformation.

Cancer takes us through many dark valleys, but it can also push us to the top of the mountain where everything becomes crystal clear. There is nothing that can compare to the joy that is to be found in that hilltop hour.

Dear God, remind me as I traverse the dark valleys of cancer and even as I walk through the valley of the shadow of death, that there will be a hilltop hour. Ease my dark days with visions of the bright ones to come. And help me to remember always that You are beside me in the dark valleys even as You will be there to celebrate with me in my hilltop hour.

~ Amen ~

Finding Meaning in Our Grief

• • • *W*hen we finally know we are dying, and all other sentient beings are dying with us, we start to have a burning, almost heartbreaking sense of the fragility and preciousness of each moment and each being, and from this can grow a deep, clear, limitless compassion for all beings. ~ Sogyal Rinpoche

Those of us who battle cancer are usually so focused on that disease and every news item that suggests a new treatment alternative, vaccine or – dare we say it? – cure that we are often startled out of that world by news of other tragedies: three young soldiers, barely out of their teens, are killed by a roadside bomb in Iraq; a toddler is killed by a falling tree limb on a sunny spring afternoon; a healthy young woman suffers a stroke during childbirth and dies as her baby takes his first breath; a doctor who devoted his life to healing others is killed when a bicycle and an automobile collide.

I learned of all of these tragic deaths within the last week. The families and friends are, of course, inconsolable, confused and angry, as we all would be. Our prayers go out to them as we struggle to find words that might ease their suffering, even if just a little.

As heartbreaking as they are and as unspeakably agonizing for the families and friends of those who died, these terrible losses can – given time and care and the opportunity for reflection – serve to remind us that our mortality is not a burden we must bear or a punishment we must live our lives dreading. Our mortality is, in fact, a gift, for if we were immortal, if we knew we would never die, our lives would have no meaning.

Instead, in the years to come, the friends and families affected by the tragic deaths described above will celebrate the lives of their loved ones in ways that share the meaning of their lives with others. The soldiers' names will become a part of our nation's history, and the legacy of these young lives will be the freedom of the country and the people for whom they fought and died. Perhaps the parents of the child who was killed by the falling tree limb will start a foundation in her memory to aid other grieving parents or raise funds to build a new wing on the hospital where medical professionals fought to save her life. Maybe the husband of the young woman who died in childbirth will form a support group for single fathers, and perhaps the son will be so inspired by the sacrifice his mother made to give him life that he will devote his life to saving others. The colleagues of the doctor whose life was taken so suddenly might create a meditation garden on the hospital grounds, a place of peace and thanksgiving where his patients and their families and all who loved him can find comfort and solitude. These are just a few of the ways that those of us who grieve can find purpose and meaning in our grief while honoring those we have lost.

During my cancer experience, I cringed when people said, "Don't worry. God won't give you more than you can handle." The fact of the matter is that sometimes people do get more than they can handle, and God didn't give them any of it. I believe in a God who is a gentle, loving father. Gentle, loving fathers don't hurt and kill their children. God didn't give me cancer any more than He directed a madman to plant that roadside bomb, broke off that tree limb and allowed it to fall on a little child, burst a vessel in the young mother's brain or caused the collision that took the doctor's life. Such tragedies are caused by biological glitches, horrific accidents and man's inhumanity to man.

Instead, God has given us many amazing gifts, two of which I consider the most precious: the first is the gift of our mortality so that we might live each day with passion and joy, knowing that our days are limited in number, and the second is the gift of one another, for it is in one another – our friends, colleagues, family members and other loved ones – that we find comfort for our aching hearts, courage for the dark nights, and strength for the journey.

The following was read at my own brother's funeral. I have found great comfort in it and hope that you will also:

"Death is nothing at all. I have only slipped away into the next room. I am I, and you are you. Whatever we were to each other, that we still are. Call me by my old familiar name, speak to me in the easy way which you always used. Put no difference in your tone, wear no forced air of solemnity or sorrow. Laugh as we always laughed at the little jokes we enjoyed together. Pray, smile, think of me, pray for me. Let my name be ever the household word that it always was. Let it be spoken

without effect, without the trace of a shadow on it.
Life means all that it ever meant. It is the same as it
ever was; there is unbroken continuity. Why should I
be out of mind because I am out of sight? I am waiting
for you, for an interval, somewhere very near, just
round the corner. All is well."

Henry Scott Holland
(1847- 1918)
Canon of St. Paul's Cathedral

Survival is a form of resistance.

Mendel Le Sueur

Forgiveness

orgiveness is the fragrance the violet sheds on the heel that has crushed it.

~Author Unknown

  Friends had told me for years that the anger and bitterness I carried around inside me were hurting no one but me. I didn't believe them and, even if they were right, I didn't care. After all, I reasoned, didn't the people who were the objects of my fury deserve it? Hadn't they created chaos in my life, hurt people I loved and left a swath of mayhem and destruction?

  Yes, I was sure they deserved my anger, and I believed I had earned the right to carry it around with me, kind of like a medal of some kind. In some distorted way (I now realize), it gave me a sense of power over the objects of my bitter feelings. Surely they could sense how I felt about them, and surely I was getting even with them by sending those bad vibes their way.

  Then I got cancer.

  Now, don't get me wrong. I'm not saying I got cancer because I was bitter and angry. It isn't quite that simple. As we all know, there may be a number of contributing factors in any cancer diagnosis, and in some cases there is no contributing factor that anyone can identify.

  But stay with me a minute and check this out. According to the American Academy of Family Physicians, "Your body responds to the way you think, feel and act. This is often called the 'mind/body connection.' When you are stressed, anxious or upset, your body tries to tell you that something isn't right. Back pain, a change in appetite, chest pain, constipation or diarrhea, heart palpitations – any one of these and a whole host of other symptoms can signal that your emotional health, and thus your mind/body connection, is out of balance."

The AAFP also tells us that poor emotional health can weaken the body's immune system, "making it more likely to get colds and other infections during emotionally difficult times." It stands to reason, then, that if you carry negative feelings around inside you *for years and years* (thus creating for yourself "emotionally difficult times" that never end, resulting in steadily eroding emotional health), you are greatly weakening your immune system over time, leaving your body vulnerable to more numerous and more serious conditions and diseases.

I read a lot about the mind/body connection after my cancer diagnosis, and I figured something out early on in the treatment and recovery process: I needed to work on my emotional health, and a big part of that meant forgiving several people who had hurt me and letting go of all the anger and bitterness I felt toward them. But how?

I began by attending an afternoon retreat with several friends who also felt the need to forgive people in their lives. The retreat was held at a nearby religious sanctuary, but what we did there can be done just as easily in your own home.

Under the guidance of two nuns, our small group created a ritual of forgiveness. We lit candles and put on some soft music, and one of the sisters built a fire in the big stone fireplace. We began with a prayer asking God to open our hearts to forgiveness and to help us let go of negative feelings.

Each of us then wrote letters to the people who had hurt us. We poured out all of the anger we felt, relating every detail of every painful word and deed. Some sobbed as they wrote. Several had to take breaks and walk around in order to calm down. Each of us kept to ourselves, however, not interrupting one another's experience even when we wanted to comfort or console. For the ritual to be successful, each of us had to do our own "spiritual homework," no matter how painful it might be.

When we had exhausted the negative, we turned to the positive. We wrote that we were forgiving the ones who had hurt us. We made it clear that didn't mean that what they had done to us was okay. It only meant we were letting go of our feelings about them in order to begin healing our own minds, spirits and bodies.

When we had finished writing, we destroyed the letters by throwing them into the fireplace. Each of us then wrote just the first names of the people we needed and wanted to forgive on a small slip of paper. With these slips in our hands, we prayed for them by name. We asked God to bless them and to release us from feelings of hurt and anger. Then we put the slips of paper into a small metal urn and touched a lit match to them. They were gone in an instant.

I won't claim that I've never had another negative feeling about the people I focused on that day, and there have even been one or two new people in my life who have wreaked havoc for a time. But I will tell you that every time I have had a negative thought or feeling about any of them, I was instantly aware of it and made myself stop immediately. I then blessed that person, forgave him anew, and released the negative energy.

Father, You forgive all, and I know You want me
to forgive, too, but I'm a mere mortal and it is so hard.
You alone know how deep are my wounds, how agonizing
the hurt, how debilitating the scars. Please teach me to
forgive those who have hurt me. Show me the way to
release myself from bitterness and anger, God, so that
I might begin to heal in mind, spirit and body.
~ Amen ~

God will only mend a broken heart
when He is given all the pieces.

Unknown

When it seems that our sorrow is too great to be borne, let us think of the great family of the heavy-hearted into which our grief has given us entrance, and inevitably, we will feel about us their arms and their understanding.

Helen Keller

Learning to Live in the Moment

I f we could see the miracle of a single flower clearly, our whole life would change.

~Gautama Siddharta

Regardless of our diagnoses and prognoses, learning to live in the moment can remarkably alter the way we spend our remaining days on this earth, granting us joy and peace in the very time and place we believed them to be impossible.

The first step is to consciously let go of the past. Stop beating yourself up over what may or may not have caused your disease. We need to remember that in many cases, there are no answers to the riddles of disease. Many people who have taken incredibly good care of themselves all of their lives get cancer and other serious illnesses, too. We need to let go of the obsession many of us have with finding out why we got cancer. And if we imagine that it is something we did or didn't do, we need to forgive ourselves.

Secondly, we must refuse to be overwhelmed by worries about tomorrow. This is perhaps hardest of all when facing a life crisis, but it *can* be done and you *can* do it, but it *does* take practice. Do you have surgery tomorrow? Chemotherapy treatment? Radiation? Other painful or frightening procedure or test? Focusing on it today will not put it off or make it go away, but it *will* rob you of the potential joys in today. *Find them!* I find joy in watching a favorite old movie for the hundredth time, going through family photos, indulging in cheesecake and painting with watercolors, but you are the only one who knows what brings you joy. Give yourself the gift of joy in the moments of today, and let tomorrow take care of tomorrow.

We can take a lesson from those recovering from the illness of addiction, those who remind themselves and one another that we can only live our lives "one day at a time." There are even days when we can only endure an hour at a time, even one minute at a time, but the minutes and the hours and the days endured are victories in and of themselves. They are battles won, and they are to be celebrated joyously. These are the moments that add up to the sums of our lives.

Resolve to celebrate every morning that you open your eyes, every contact with a loved one, every moment that you draw breath, the breath itself, every seemingly inconsequential thing or occurrence which, if examined closely, reveals a miracle.

When you temporarily lose your resolve, don't give up. Remind yourself that this is a new approach that requires practice, and gently return your attention to the present moment. If you can focus on this task and make it a conscious practice each and every day, its promise is that the joyful moments will greatly outweigh the sorrowful ones when the sums of our lives are tallied.

Dear God, I've been awfully hard on myself lately,
blaming myself for mistakes real and imagined, and
convincing myself that they are the reasons I have cancer.
I often obsess over what tomorrow will bring and how

many tomorrows I have left. Please help me get past this harmful thinking. Help me in my resolve to build healthy new habits, to forgive myself for my old unhealthy ones, and to live joyously in the moment every moment for all the rest of my days.

~ Amen ~

Learn to get in touch with silence within yourself and know that everything in this life has a purpose. There are no mistakes, no coincidences. All events are blessings given to us to learn from.

Elisabeth Kübler-Ross

Life After Cancer

Courage is the price that life exacts for granting peace.
~Amelia Earhart

When I received my cancer diagnosis, what I wanted more than anything in the world was to meet, talk to and hopefully get a hug from long-term cancer survivors.

One of my happiest moments during that awful time was the evening I met a woman who was a 7-year cancer survivor. She hugged me and told me I would be fine, and I believed her. Now, of course I knew in my head that all cancers are different and that, in all likelihood, she had had totally different treatments for her cancer than I had for mine, but the facts didn't matter to me right then.

What mattered was that another human being who had been through pretty much the same thing I was going through – and, more importantly, someone who knew the raw terror I was experiencing – was still standing, proof that I could come out on the other side of this. She was hugging me and infusing me with her strength and her courage and her humanity. She made me believe what all of my doctors' reassurances and the nurses' encouraging words had not been able to because she spoke to my heart.

But there was something she didn't tell me, something that every cancer survivor learns at some point, something I'm going to share with you now, and that is this: cancer changes our lives in many ways, and it changes our lives *forever*.

Most of the ways are good. Nearly every cancer survivor we've ever met agrees that the cancer experience has given them a richer, deeper appreciation for life and pushed them to live their lives with greater joy than they ever knew before cancer.

On the flip side, we cancer survivors will forever be getting those extra special checkups on a regular basis. We will be nervous, often scared, occasionally terrified. Some of us have to go through these examinations every few months for years, some more often and some less frequently.

Many long-term survivors find that, the further out from diagnosis they get, the more they run into a particular problem. The problem is that the people who weren't around them during their illness and who have only known them with hair and rosy cheeks and bright eyes just don't get it. We have even heard from some long-term survivors that people have said to them, "You look so healthy. You must not have had a very bad kind of cancer" (Excuse me? There are good kinds?). In other cases, new and/or casual acquaintances have actually implied that a long-term survivor never really had cancer at all!

We've heard from several long-term survivors who've encountered problems with employers and co-workers who think the survivor is using his medical history as an excuse to take a few days off when he is due for check-ups and follow-up tests.

When a work-related situation arises, it is absolutely necessary to take action in order to avoid discriminatory treatment. Ask your oncologist to speak with your employer if it seems to be a simple matter of lack of understanding. In more serious cases, it may be necessary to contact someone who can act as an advocate on your behalf. Many oncology practices and hospitals have such patient advocates on staff; if they don't, they can put you in touch with advocates in your community. In the most serious cases where real workplace discrimination is taking place, it becomes necessary to contact an attorney.

For the most part, however, the simple answer to these concerns is that it is up to us to educate the public. It is up to us as survivors to teach people who might otherwise never know it that there are more than 10 million cancer survivors in this country and we walk among them every day. Our hair has grown back and our cheeks glow and our eyes sparkle. We go to work and we go to school and we get married and we have babies and we live our lives just like everyone else. The differences between us and everyone else are generally unseen (medications, medical appliances, etc.), and every now and then we have to call upon every ounce of courage we can muster and go have some scary tests to make sure everything is okay.

If you find yourself in a situation where someone is implying that you couldn't have been very sick, if in fact you were ever sick at all, and that you might be a bit of a hypochondriac, remind yourself that you don't owe that person or anyone else any explanations. You don't owe anyone anything. You've paid your dues and then some. You're a survivor, a champion, a warrior, the very definition of courage and determination. And that is something no one can ever take away from you.

Bless the person who suggests anything different, and move on.

Dear God, Please help me move forward with my life, ever mindful that I am changed now, for the better and forever. Be with me as I lie on the examining table, undergo frightening and sometimes painful tests, and as I endure the seemingly endless wait for results. When others are less than kind about the differences between them and me, help me to remember that this is only between You and me. Give me the strength to bless them, turn away and face only You.

~ Amen ~

There is in every heart a spark of heavenly fire which lies dormant in the broad daylight of prosperity, but which kindles up and beams and blazes in the dark hour of adversity.

Washington Irving

There is a light in this world, a healing spirit more powerful than any darkness we may encounter. We sometimes lose sight of this force when there is suffering, and too much pain. Then suddenly, the spirit will emerge through the lives of ordinary people who hear a call and answer in extraordinary ways.

Mother Teresa

Post Office Epiphany

The life I touch for good or ill will touch another life, and that in turn another, until who knows where the trembling stops or in what far place my touch will be felt. ~ Frederick Buechner

Before cancer, many of us go through life pretty clueless. I know I did. I worried about things that seem trivial now: a petty difference with a co- worker, irritation over a spill on the carpet, too many things to do and too few hours in the day to do them. I spent my days running around and making myself crazy over the smallest details.

After my diagnosis and throughout most of my treatment, I went back and forth from borderline hysteria to resignation and depression.

Then one day, for the first time in many months, I was feeling physically strong enough to take on a few errands by myself. I went to the post office to buy stamps.

As I stood in the long line – a little weak in the knees, bedraggled wig on my head, painted-on eyebrows and no lashes, and more than a bit queasy in the stomach – I began to feel rather proud of myself. I thought *I have been through so much in the last year. I have been sicker than I ever thought a human being could be and still be alive, but here I am. I'm still standing, I'm doing things for myself again and, hey, this feels pretty good!*

Then I noticed that two women ahead of me were becoming very agitated and vocal about the long, slow-moving line. They began complaining loudly that they had "better things to do than wait in line at the post office all day."

I thought about that for a minute and then asked myself *Do I have anything better to do today than what I'm doing right this minute? Do I have anything better to do than just be alive and grateful?* And then the answer: *Nope.*

That's when it happened. I felt myself begin to glow. Today I tell people that it was either an epiphany or the mother of all hot flashes (what we in the South call "private summers"), but whatever it was, it was powerful and life-altering. So I just stood there, basking in its warmth, and I slowly began to understand some important truths: This moment is all I have. And in this moment, there is nothing I really *have* to do except breathe in, breathe out and say "Thank you!"

I wanted to say something to the two women. I wanted to ask them if they had any idea how lucky they were to be *able* to stand there in that line, if they knew how many people would gladly change places with them, if they even had a *clue* what a priceless gift it is to be able to stand in a line and buy stamps all by yourself! But of course I didn't.

Many people argue that there is nothing good that comes of the cancer experience. I disagree. I believe that, if we allow it to, cancer can bring us many gifts. One of the gifts of cancer is the gift of patience. I no longer "sweat the small stuff." I don't allow petty differences with co-workers to even happen. If there are people who are confrontational or negative, I can choose to keep my distance from them. A spill on the carpet is laughable. My response to most things is, "So what? In the grand scheme of things, how important is it really?" Most of the time, the answer is that it's not important at all.

Dear God, help me to remember that this moment
is all that any of us has, whether we are cancer
survivors or not. Our lives are in Your hands, and every
day we are alive is a gift filled with new possibilities and
opportunities. All we have to do is open Your "present."
And please help me to remember that there
is nothing I have to do that is more important than
breathing in and breathing out and thanking you for
the fact that I am alive today.
~ Amen ~

Sorrows come to stretch out spaces
in the heart – for joy.

Edwin Markham

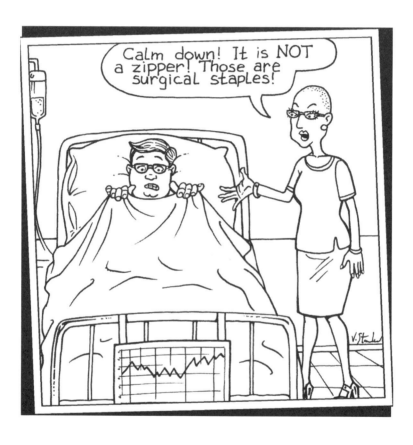

Seasons

Your pain is the breaking of the shell that encloses your understanding. Even as the stone of the fruit must break, that its heart may stand in the sun, so must you know pain. And could you keep your heart in wonder at the daily miracles of your life, your pain would not seem less wondrous than your joy. And you would accept the seasons of your heart, even as you have always accepted the seasons that pass over your fields. And you would watch with serenity through the winters of your grief. ~ Kahlil Gibran

My chemotherapy and radiation treatments were finally over, and I had begun the long, slow process of physical, emotional and spiritual healing.

My older son had graduated from high school and joined the United States Marine Corps. Initially I was disappointed that he had not chosen to go to college right away, and of course I was worried for his safety, but I was also immensely proud of his decision and his courage.

During his training at Parris Island, he sent me a letter describing some of what he was experiencing. He told of the biting sand fleas that infested the camp. He told of ten-mile training runs in sweltering heat and humidity and the resulting blisters on his feet that broke and bled. He told of taking a pounding from another recruit in a boxing exercise.

The most amazing thing about the letter, however, was that not one word of my son's detailed account held even a hint of complaint! He was clearly (and deservedly) proud of himself and his fellow recruits and marveling each and every day at how much discomfort and even excruciating pain they could withstand.

The letter ended with these words: "Mom, remember that pain is just weakness leaving your body."

What powerful words those were! I clung to them and made them my mantra. I wrote them on an index card and taped it where I could see it every day.

Cancer treatment is never pleasant. Much of the time it's pretty awful. My own experience was like that of most other cancer patients in that I had some degree of nausea or pain (or both) on most days. There were many days when all I could do was hang on and hope the next one would be better.

But with the words of my son's letter and the attitude they mirrored, the way in which I looked at my pain and nausea shifted. They no longer meant that I was deathly ill. They meant that I was alive and that weakness and disease were leaving my body.

From the day I received that letter to this very minute, I have found discomfort and pain of every kind to be easier to bear if I just remind myself of my son's brave words and courageous spirit.

God, with Your help, I will see the side effects of my treatments as my body's way of getting rid of cancer. I will remember that pain means I'm alive. And when I am most tired and sick, I will remember that this illness is just another of the seasons of my life, and that winter always gives way to spring.

~ Amen ~

When we are mindful, deeply in touch with the present moment, our understanding of what is going on deepens, and we begin to be filled with acceptance, joy, peace and love.

Thich Nhat Hanh

Scars and Stars

*L*ife is not a journey to the grave with the intention
of arriving safely in a pretty, well-preserved body,
but rather to skid in broadside, thoroughly used
up, totally worn out, and loudly proclaiming, "Wow!
What a ride!"   ~ Author Unknown

In an interview on "Larry King Live" on August 23 of
last year, musician Sheryl Crow discussed her recent bout
with breast cancer and the radiation treatments she underwent. She pointed to a tiny dark speck visible just above
the neckline of her blouse and explained that it was one of
several tattoos that were applied to help guide the radiation
technicians as they administered her treatments. She commented that, "Ultimately, I might get (them) removed," but
went on to say she would keep the tattoos for the time being
so that she wouldn't be too quick to forget the powerful life
lesson she had just experienced.

I was a little taken aback when she said that she might
one day have her tattoos removed. I've had mine for eleven
years now. I wouldn't give them up for anything because
it's not in the short term that we are in danger of forgetting
the lessons cancer has to teach us, but rather in the long
term. It is now – in these days long removed from daily trips
to the hospital, seemingly endless rounds of chemotherapy,
and surgery after surgery after surgery – that I need to see
those tiny blue dots when I undress. It is now – when life

is good and I am strong and tempted sometimes to pretend that I never had cancer – that I need to touch them and re-member, not with sadness and fear, but with joy and pride in what I endured and overcame. I've never thought of having them removed, but I have considered having one of them transformed into a tiny butterfly, a symbol of triumph and rebirth.

Think long and hard, Sheryl, before you have your radiation tattoos removed. Celebrate not only those tiny marks, but also every scar, every mark, every wrinkle to come in the days and years ahead because each of them tells and will tell a piece of the story of who you are. They are part of your music, precious notes in the song that is your life.

A subscriber named Lyn recently wrote to us the following message: "I know someone who is so horrified by her little blue radiation tattoos that she is planning to have them removed. On the other hand, I have wondered what constellation I would get if I connected my dots."

Stars! She sees them as stars on her body!

What a gift she gave me with those words. Maybe instead of a butterfly, I'll get a tiny star...

Dear God, Remind me not to be ashamed of my scars, but to see them as stars in my constellation, brushstrokes in the masterpiece that is my life.
~ Amen ~

Cancer can take away all my physical abilities. It cannot touch my mind, it cannot touch my heart and it cannot touch my soul. And those three things are going to carry on forever.

Jim Valvano

The Cancer Crusade on Vacation.

The Tale of the Whale

I t is a wholesome and necessary thing for us to turn
again to the earth and in the contemplation of her
beauties to know of wonder and humility.

~ Rachel Carson

According to an article that appeared in the *San Francisco
Chronicle* on December 14, 2005, crab fishermen working
just east of the Farallone Islands spotted a female humpback
whale that had become entangled in a web of crab traps and
lines. She was weighted down by hundreds of pounds of traps,
and she had hundreds of yards of line rope wrapped around
her body, tail and torso, and a line tugging in her mouth. The
majestic creature was struggling mightily to stay on the sur-
face so she could breathe, but her situation was desperate.

Experts assessed the situation and concluded the whale's
only chance for survival rested with a team of marine rescuers who would need to get into the water with her and
cut her bonds one by one. This was an extremely danger-
ous venture because any thrashing on the part of the 50-ton
animal could be deadly to the rescuers. One slap of her tail
could kill a diver.

One of the divers, James Moskito, said the whale was
peaceful during the hour or so it took the team of rescuers to
cut the ropes, and that there was a "vibration" coming from
the whale the entire time. Moskito said that when the whale

realized she was free, she began swimming in what seemed to be "joyous" circles. "It felt to me like she was thanking us, knowing that she was free and that we had helped her," Moskito said. "She stopped about a foot away from me, pushed me around a little bit and had some fun." He said the whale nuzzled him, then swam to each of the other rescuers and nuzzled them as well. Others on the team said it was the most "incredibly beautiful experience" of their lives. The diver who cut the rope from her mouth said her eye followed him while he worked, and he "will never be the same."

When I was undergoing treatment for cancer, there were days when I could hardly move from my bed. I needed help to do the simplest of things like getting dressed, bathing, going to the bathroom. It was humiliating. At age 44, I had always been healthy, strong and independent. This, I thought at the time, was the absolute worst, and for a time I became angry and sullen.

Well, it wasn't the absolute worst. *That* came a few weeks later when I couldn't do *anything* for myself. I had been reduced to complete and total helplessness. I had no choice but to lie still and let others care for me.

As I lay on the couch one day, I watched my mother carry laundry downstairs, smelled the vegetable soup she was cooking in the kitchen, listened to the sound of the lawn mower outside as my son cut the grass, and saw my husband bent over the dining room table as he paid our bills. A friend stopped by with the prescription she had picked up for me. The mail brought a cheery card from church friends and a sur-prise package from my aunt. A cousin called from a thousand miles away just to remind me that I was in her prayers.

Suddenly, a powerful wave of emotion washed over me. I was literally stunned into silence. Unlike anything I had ever felt before, it was a mix of gratitude and love and humility and a thousand other feelings I couldn't identify. I realized in what Oprah calls a "lightbulb moment" how much my family and friends love me.

Of course I'd heard them tell me that hundreds of times over the years. Our family and many of our friends say "I love you" to one another dozens of times a day. But now I was *seeing* that love in action. It was an awesome thing to see, and I am forever changed...and blessed.

I know what that whale must have felt as she watched her rescuers care for her. My family and friends "untangled" me from the ropes and lines that temporarily weighed me down. They were my rescuers, caring for me at a time when I could not care for myself.

Today, eleven years later, I often run around in circles (okay, *walk* around in circles – hey, I'm 55 now!) just for the sheer joy of being alive in this moment, *today*, *right now*, and the knowledge that I am so blessed to love and be loved.

These are truly the greatest gifts of all.

Dear God, keep me ever mindful of the love that surrounds me. When I am angry at my disease, let me not take it out on those who care for me. Remind me to be silent and still so that I can observe and absorb the deep and abiding love of those who are there to lend a hand in these difficult days. Open my eyes to the wonder of Your gifts of family and friends. Thank You, thank You, thank You, God, for the awesome miracles of loving and being loved!

~ Amen ~

The idea of taking charge of
one's medical program is the single
most common practice among
survivors. It is the cornerstone of
a strategic recovery plan.

Greg Anderson

Special Messages for Caregivers

A Friend in Need Is a Friend Indeed

by Deedra Miller

L ove will enter cloaked in friendship's name.
~ Ovid

My daughter was diagnosed with cancer in September, 2004. There was such an outpouring of support and so many people wanted to help that, after a while, it actually became something of a problem. We didn't want to hurt people's feelings, but all we could think of was what was going on at the hospital. With the shock of the diagnosis and so much uncertainty about the future, we really didn't know what we would need, but as time went by, and through much trial and error, we came up with a list of a few things that really helped us out.

- Play with our pets. We spent a lot of time at the hospital, and even when we were home, we were pre-occupied. We asked a neighbor to spend some time playing with our dogs and giving them attention.

- Pick up the mail.

- Decorate our house for the holidays. I did not have the time or the energy, but when I put out the boxes for different holidays, my friends came over and put the decorations up. Later they took them down and put them away. It really lifted our spirits to come home from the hospital and see our decorations up. At a time when we felt we were missing out on so much, this made us feel like we were still a part of the holiday seasons. On Halloween, we had pumpkins on our porch. On Valentine's Day, there were hearts hanging from a tree.

- Deliver meals. One friend was the contact and she made a schedule and gave people food ideas (foods we liked, and not too many lasagnas in one month). We kept a cooler on the front porch so people could put the meals in it. This way we could keep germs out, and if we were busy or resting, we didn't feel obligated to visit. There were markers in the cooler so people could sign it (or you could put a pen and pad inside for people to leave notes).

- Take care of our plants (inside and out). It's no fun to see things dying.

- Remember the kids (siblings or children). People sent our son gift cards. This reminded him that others understood this had changed his life, too.

- Donate items. Friends brought those household items that are convenient to have on hand: laundry soap, paper towels, paper plates, disinfectant wipes, etc. Other thoughtful gifts included gas cards, restaurant cards and video rentals.

- Help with cleaning. Some people don't want their friends to see their "dirty laundry," so they turn down offers of help with housework. Several Sunday school classes at our church took turns hiring a maid service for us. We loved it!

It's also important for friends and family to respect the wishes of the patient and his family when they say they don't want certain types of help. Maybe they don't know what they want. It doesn't help when others put pressure on them to come up with something.

The patient and his family may feel like they've lost so much control that they don't want others to do everything for them. They don't want to feel like they've lost control of everything, so sometimes it's best not to push them into coming up with ways for you to help.

It really helped us when someone offered to do one of the above because they were things that could be done without us having to sit there and feel incapable. It's really hard to sit and watch others take care of you, and it can make you feel guilty. That's not the point of helping. The point is to simply and quietly make the patient and his family's life a little better.

Dear God, we are so blessed to have many friends and family members who want to help us during this difficult time, but sometimes their generosity and questions about what we need can give us even more to worry about. Remind those who care for us that taking care of simple chores and supplying everyday necessities can be the kindest gifts of all.

~ Amen ~

Heroes take journeys, confront dragons, and discover the treasure of their true selves.

Carol Pearson

A Message for Those Who Grieve

*T*he deeper that sorrow carves into your being the more joy you can contain. Is not the cup that holds your wine the very cup that was burned in the potter's oven?   ~ Kahlil Gibran

We recently received an e-mail message from a woman whose sister had passed away after a long battle with cancer.

"During (my sister's) battle," she wrote, "I found it easy to talk with others diagnosed with cancer. (She) displayed such incredible and amazing inspiration that encouragement came easily; I simply shared her walk!...(But now) I have become awkward and impotent to encourage. It's horrible. I hate that I find myself unable to pass on her strength and zest/appreciation for each day. Each time I have tried, the question always comes, 'How is your sister?'"

She then asked if we would address her concern in one of our weekly affirmations. Knowing it is a concern that many face, we thought that was an excellent idea, and so we are sharing our response with all of our readers:

What you are experiencing is very common. In fact, it is the expected reaction to a loss such as you've experienced. This is the time to focus on yourself and your own healing. You need to give yourself some time. How much? It's different for everyone. Don't rush. Be gentle with yourself. Your spirit will know when it's ready to move forward. In the meantime, you might want to put some distance between yourself and those who are fighting cancer. Just for now. Just until you feel ready.

When that time comes, you may find that you want to become more involved in the war on cancer, and you may find that you want to become less involved, and *either one is okay*. That's very important to remember! If you want to become more involved, you will likely find that your sister guides your decisions and your words when speaking with cancer patients. You will probably find that you can smile and hold their hands and encourage them with the same kind of spirit that led your sister during her journey. You will say in response to their questions, "Sadly, my sister passed away, but please remember that no two cases are ever the same."

You will remind them that new drugs are being discovered and treatment protocols are improving every single day. For example, about six years ago, a friend of ours was diagnosed with a rare type of cancer that was almost always fatal. Her doctor made it clear that she should go home and get her affairs in order. Only a few days later, he called and told her about a clinical trial for a new drug that might prolong her life and asked if she wanted to participate. Of course she did, and today she continues to be in remission. The trial drug she was on is now standard treatment for the type of cancer with which she was diagnosed, and the mortality rate for that cancer has fallen dramatically.

You may find that you want to become more involved in the fight against cancer, but are still not comfortable in one-on-one conversations with patients, and that's okay, too. If that's the case, we recommend getting involved in the American Cancer Society's "Relay For Life." It's a team-based fundraising event that culminates in one big family-friendly overnight party, usually at a local sports stadium. You can find the one nearest you by visiting the American Cancer Society's website at www.cancer.org.

Please know, too, that if you want to have nothing whatsoever to do with the whole subject of cancer, then that's the right decision for you. Throw yourself into something you've always wanted to do. Go somewhere you've always wanted to go. Learn something you've always wanted to learn. These are wonderful ways to celebrate your sister's memory because you will be moving forward and really *living* every moment of your own life! And without even knowing your sister, we feel confident that's what she would want you to do.

Dear God, Please show me the way to move through my grief, and light my path as I struggle to find my way to the other side. And when I'm there, Lord, show me what You would have me do with my own life as I celebrate that of the one whose loss I grieve and honor my loved one's memory.

~ Amen ~

Cancer Etiquette 101

*S*ometimes you feel other people's pain worse than your own. We're armored against our own troubles. We can't afford to give in to despair. Then you see someone else struggling, and it breaks your... heart.

~ Sean Stewart

What do you say when you learn that someone you care about has cancer? What do you do? Is there any "right" way or "wrong" way to respond to the news?

Most cancer survivors we've talked with have stories to tell of comments and gestures made by friends and family members, some of which were hurtful and some of which were helpful. Based on those survivors' stories as well as our own experiences, we offer the following "do's" and "don't's."

First the "don't's":

1. The worst thing you can say or do is to say or do nothing at all. Almost every survivor we've ever spoken with can tell of at least one person who, upon hearing the news, disappeared and was never heard from again. Maybe the fact that your friend or loved one has cancer is the worst news you've ever heard and you can't stand the thought of him being this sick. You don't know what to say or do, and it's too painful to see him without hair,

and the house smells like a hospital, and, well, it's all so just so scary. We don't mean to be harsh here, but this really isn't about you. Stick around, please. Your loving presence alone can be the healing salve for a wounded, frightened spirit.

2. We know you mean well when you say, "God won't give you more than you can handle," but we wish you would listen to the implications in that comment and refrain from using it. It implies that God gave us cancer which inference often leads newly diagnosed patients to wonder if God is punishing them for something they did or failed to do, and that's the last thing we need to be worrying about right now.

To clean up a popular phrase, stuff happens. People get cancer (1 in 3, in fact). People get lots of other awful diseases, too. Babies are born with defects. Long-distance runners have heart attacks. Brave men and women go to war and get killed. Supermen fall from horses, and maniacs fly airplanes into buildings. And, yes, many people do get more than they can handle as evidenced by suicide rates. We don't mean to step on anyone's religion here, but we refuse to believe God is the one causing all this mayhem, destruction and chaos.

Conversely, we believe God grieves with us when these things happen, and He is there for us and with us in the treatment room, in the delivery room, on the racecourse, on the battlefield, in the emergency room, on the airplane and inside its target. Instead of telling us that God gave us cancer, tell us that God will be with us every step of the way.

3. Don't try to predict our future. Acknowledge the seriousness of the diagnosis without being morbid ("Oh, my God! My aunt had the very same thing and she died 8 months later!") and without being unrealistic ("You'll probably outlive me. I could get hit by a bus tomorrow!"). We don't know what's going to happen to us, and neither do you. Tell us happy stories of other long-term cancer survivors (but refrain from saying someone had "the very same thing"; no two cancer diagnoses are ever the same). *Never, ever tell us stories with unhappy endings.*

Now for the "do's":

1. Things to say: "I'm here for you." "You can cry with me." "I love you." "I won't leave you." "Whatever you're feeling is okay." Just be there. Follow our lead. We'll let you know if we want to "talk about it," and if we do, please let us. Don't change the subject. When you don't allow us to talk about our disease, it makes us feel alone and isolated.

2. Things to do: Take my kids out for pizza and a movie or, better yet, for the weekend. Offer to pick up prescriptions, take the dog to the groomer and run other errands. Clip cartoons and funny pictures and send them in a card. Bring thoughtful gifts (a book or magazine, a tabletop fountain, a meditation tape or CD); avoid things with strong smells (bath sets, flowers, food, etc.) until you know how I'm reacting to my treatments.

    A special message for doctors and other medical professionals: We know there are no guarantees, but you can give us hope. Your patients ask you for hope in different ways. Some are subtle, and some are screaming. Remember that where there is life, there is hope, and *remind us of that*. Instead of just saying, "You have cancer, and it's very serious," say, "You have cancer. It's very serious, but once you get past the shock of this diagnosis, you are going to discover what a strong, resilient person you are. That strength and resilience partnered with our staff's knowledge, skill and experience are going to form a powerful team to fight this disease. We're going to do this together."

Dear God, someone I love has cancer. I am so afraid for him, and I don't know what to say or do to ease his pain and fear. Help me today to become a true caregiver in every sense of the word. Let my mouth speak only words of comfort and hope. Let my hands lend warmth and strength. Let everything I say and do be helpful, not hurtful. Guide me, God, as I walk this path with my friend. Be a lamp unto our feet as the way is often dark, and bring us into Your healing light.

~ Amen ~

Cancer got me over unimportant fears, like getting old.

Olivia Newton-John

About Courage

*C*ourage doesn't always roar. Sometimes courage is the little voice at the end of the day that says I'll try again tomorrow. ~ Mary Anne Radmacher

I was feeling pretty low the day I received my third chemotherapy treatment. I had lost all of my hair by then and was experiencing a number of other unpleasant side effects. The future was so uncertain, and I was frightened and sad.

As I sat in the reclining chair in the oncology clinic with the infusion dripping into my chest catheter, a few tears rolled down my face. One of the nurses walked by and said to me, "Don't be such a baby."

I was humiliated and angry, but – worst of all – even sadder than before. Now I felt like a failure, too. It took a long time and the loving counsel of family and friends to recover from the nurse's unkind words.

I wish I could say the following to every member of the medical community who comes in contact with cancer patients:

"Please do not judge your patients' reactions to their diseases and treatments. No matter in how many surgeries you have assisted, no matter how many infusions you have monitored, no matter how many radiation treatments you have administered, no matter *what* you have witnessed, unless you yourself have had a diagnosis of cancer, you have no idea the degree of terror and despair this news can bring.

And, if you find yourself becoming irritated by the

emotional outbursts of your patients and you feel your compassion fading, it's time for you to take a break. You need a vacation at the very least. At most, you might need to consider a career change."

That nurse should have said something along these lines: "I know you're frightened, and it's okay. Cancer treatment is scary. But you are courageous because you are here today getting your treatment. I admire you because you are moving forward and not allowing yourself to be paralyzed by fear. And by doing these things, you are optimizing your chances of recovery."

It seems like we always think later of the perfect comeback, what we "should have said" in a situation like the one I've described here. I'm going to give it to you now so that you will have it ready should anyone feel qualified to comment on your fears, tears, worries, frustrations or sadness with anything less than the utmost compassion.

Just say firmly, "I'm here, aren't I?"

Dear God, help me to remember that it's okay to cry. And when I do, help me to feel Your comforting arms around me and to know that, no matter what happens, I am safe in Your care. Help me to remember that You are proud of me because I am moving forward in spite of the fact that I am afraid. I am showing up for my treatments and following my doctor's instructions. And, God, please surround the medical professionals who treat me with Your love and comfort. They are suffering, too. They witness more human pain and despair on a daily basis than most of us can even imagine. Help them to rediscover the compassionate spirits that led them to the medical profession and to see each patient in his own light and not as a reflection of others.

~ Amen ~

When Depression Strikes

God is closest to those with broken hearts.
~ Jewish Saying

I hesitated a bit to write about this dark subject, but a number of e-mail and voice messages we've received convinced me it was an important topic to address, so here goes.

The messages have been from friends and family members of those battling cancer. Each of the writers of these messages expressed concern about a patient's state of mind. They related anecdotal information such as "She doesn't want to do anything anymore" or "He won't even get out of bed although he's physically very able" or "She has lost interest in everything, even her own children." A few expressed concerns that a patient is "self-medicating" with alcohol and/or illegal drugs or abusing prescription drugs. And some letters spoke of fears for the entire family, that the children are becoming depressed, that the "well" spouse is drinking heavily or becoming abusive. In one case, the writer indicated that an adolescent in the home was becoming verbally and emotionally abusive to the parent with cancer. And in another case, the patient was talking and writing about suicide.

As we've stated many times, we are not medical professionals and don't pretend to be, but I don't think it takes a medical professional to recognize the warning signs of serious depression and to offer suggestions for caregivers and others who may be in a position of caring *about* a person with cancer even though he may not be caring *for* the person with cancer.

If you as a caregiver, relative or friend of a cancer survivor and/or his family observe symptoms such as the ones mentioned above, you need to step up and take some action to clue the family's physician.

People who observe such situations often say to themselves *It's really none of my business* or *I don't want them to be mad at me* or *If he/she is depressed, I'm sure the doctor already knows.* You could be very wrong on all of these counts, and it's my opinion that it's always better to be safe than sorry, especially when there is an individual or family in crisis. In some cases, a patient or family member can be in real danger. Assess the situation as best you can, and trust your instincts.

First of all, is there a family member who doesn't live in their home that you can speak with? Does the family have an oncology social worker? If not, does the patient's physician's office have a social worker, patient navigator or therapist on staff? These are the kinds of people who need to be made aware of the situation and brought into it as quickly as possible.

If you are unable to connect with any of the persons suggested above, you need to contact the patient's physician or other member of his medical team. This can be difficult sometimes, but if you believe the patient and/or his family members are in the midst of an unrecognized crisis, you really need to hang in there and follow through on this.

When you speak with the physician or other member of the patient's medical team, chances are the first words he will say will be, "I cannot discuss a patient with you without his written permission." He may even try to end the conversation abruptly. Don't let him! You counter with, "I'm not asking you to discuss anything. I'm not requesting any information. You do not even need to acknowledge that you know the person I'm referring to, and you do not have to say anything. Just listen. I am simply calling to give you information that I believe is important to this person's care and to his family's well-being." You then proceed to state your concerns, thank him for his time and ring off. If you've tried everything you can think of to speak directly to the patient's physician or other member of his medical team, send the physician a letter marked "Personal." You will have done what you can, and it is now the responsibility of the physician and medical team to intervene.

In the meantime, you can do your part to help by continuing to invite your friend on outings, visiting him, calling and staying in touch as much as possible. Try to engage him in activities he once enjoyed, even if only vicariously through books, magazines, videos, CD's and so forth.

Sometimes the best medicine that you as a friend or family member can offer is just sitting close and saying, "You don't have to be strong with me. You can cry with me." These words often work magic. They can help a depressed person open up and release a lot of what's going on inside, and very often that is where healing begins.

Dear God, You are our refuge in good and in bad times. In Your infinite mercy, bring peace and comfort to those of us who face days sometimes filled with pain and depression. Help us to realize that through You there is joy and the promise of lasting peace. Help us through the rough times. Walk before and beside us so that we may walk in Your footsteps and reach out to You in our journey on this earth. Help us to focus on our blessings rather than our misfortunes. Thank You for hearing and answering our prayers.

~ Amen ~

Survival, I know, is to begin again.

Judy Collins

Please visit *The Cancer Crusade's* website at

www.TheCancerCrusade.com

and sign up for the free monthly online newsletter, "The Cancer Connection," and free weekly affirmations.

And please take a few minutes to view *The Survivor Movie* at www.TheSurvivorMovie.com. This little movie has been called "the three most powerful minutes on the internet." It has been viewed more than a million times in more than 75 countries. *The Cancer Crusade* received the "Yoplait Champions Award" from Yoplait and its parent company General Mills, Susan G. Komen For The Cure and SELF magazine for the creation of *The Survivor Movie*.

Roger and Kathy Cawthon
The Cancer Crusade
P.O. Box 8139
Hampton, VA 23666
757.826.7513

Visit us: www.TheCancerCrusade.com
Write to us: cawthons@TheCancerCrusade.com

About the Authors

Roger Cawthon is a former reporter for CNN and an anchor at ABC and CBS affiliates. He has received numerous awards in the fields of broadcast journalism and business as well as from the American Cancer Society. He is a graduate of the United States Military Academy at West Point.

Kathy Cawthon is an author and photographer whose work has received numerous awards from the Virginia Press Association, National Federation of Press Women, National Education Association, American Cancer Society and Susan G. Komen For The Cure. She is a graduate of the College of William and Mary where she is also a Fellow of the Eastern Virginia Writing Project.

Roger and Kathy are both cancer survivors. Diagnosed within six weeks of each other eleven years ago, they underwent more than a year of aggressive medical treatments to which they added their own complementary therapies of faith, humor, nutrition and exercise. Roger and Kathy celebrated their survival by completing the Marine Corps Marathon four years after their diagnoses.

In 1999, they founded The Cancer Crusade, an organization dedicated to fighting cancer with hope and humor through an interactive website, free online publications, and humorous, uplifting presentations. The Cancer Crusade's online production The Survivor Movie (www.TheSurvivorMovie.com) has been called "the three most powerful minutes on the internet" and received the "2006 Yoplait Champions Award" from Yoplait, Susan G. Komen For The Cure and SELF magazine. The Cawthons were featured in a production of The Discovery Health Network and have appeared on the Today show.

They live in Virginia.